Momma, Stop! I'll Be Good!

- *Part 2 of Kevin's Story* -

Based on
a True Story of Child Abuse

By Shannon Bowen

NEW FOREST
BOOKS

Copyright

Author's statement: I have tried to recreate events, locales and conversations from my memories of them. In order to maintain their anonymity in some instances I have changed the names of individuals and places, I may have changed some identifying characteristics and details such as physical properties, occupations and places of residence.

To contact the author, visit Shannon-Bowen.com.

Other books by Shannon Bowen:

- Momma, Don't Hit Me! (The start of the Kevin story.)

- What Happened to Kevin (Both "Momma" books in a two-volume set.)

Table of Contents

Introduction

My previous book, "Momma, Don't Hit Me!" covered October 2011 to the end of September 2012.

At the time I published "Momma, Don't Hit Me!" I *thought* the story was over.

Maryann told me that Joe had full custody of Kevin, and Ann was getting ready to move out, as well. Both Maryann and I were relieved, and felt as if we could finally move on with our lives, free of worries about Kevin.

Then, Joe brought Kevin back to Ann, and things went awry.

Those unexpected twists and turns are covered in this book.

This book covers October 2012 through May 2013, and concludes Kevin's tale.

It's not a "happily ever after" ending, but it should give readers some closure to Kevin's story.

Who's Who

In this book, the people I talk about most were our next-door neighbors between October 2011 and early 2013. I've changed some personal details about the adults to protect their privacy and my own.

Kevin was a preschool child whose bedroom was on the other side of the wall from mine. He was three years old in 2011, when he and his parents moved into apartment next to ours.

Ann was his mother, whose life of excess — including drugs and prostitution — seemed certain to lead to disaster.

Joe was Kevin's father, a factory worker and former high school football star. He seemed moody, often sullen, and I struggled to believe he was oblivious to the child neglect and abuse going on right under his nose.

Maryann was the apartment manager, and my only consistent supporter as we tried to get help for Kevin.

Alphabetical list with more details

Ann was Kevin's mother. I think she's a high school dropout and, when she lived next to me, she was in her early 20s but looked much older. She appeared to be increasingly involved with drugs and prostitution.

Denise was a quiet woman and a friend of Ann and Joe. She often provided transportation for Ann, who didn't seem to drive. When Denise spent the night — for what usually looked like a threesome — Ann seemed to treat Kevin better.

Erik was the head of maintenance at our apartment complex. He's a bright, funny guy. He's married to Maryann, who was the manager of our apartment complex and the adjoining condos.

Handshake King (HK) was a cryptic young man who was part of the story — and perhaps a catalyst — during the summer of 2012. When he was here, I wasn't sure if he was an undercover police officer, a drug dealer, or neither. He was an enigma when he was here, and left a lasting impact on the community.

Henry was a regular visitor, next door. He looked about 16 years old. Briefly, in the first book, he was also Kevin's live-in babysitter. Henry seemed to have a crush on Ann, despite how she treated him. He'd been thrown out of his home when his new stepmother arrived.

Joe was Kevin's father. During this first part of the story, Joe seemed like a quiet man. He was in his early 20s, with a background in sports. He worked at the same factory as his dad did. Most of the time, he seemed very nice, but a little too worn-down by life. Later, things changed. At this point, I hope I was completely wrong about him. I hope he recovers his high school dreams, cut short by Ann's pregnancy.

Kevin was the child. He was three years old in October 2011, when this story started. When he lived next to us, he seemed bright and almost sweet at times. However, most of the time, he was a loud, out-of-control child with behavior issue. Given his home life, that's no surprise.

Maryann was the apartment manager, and a mom herself. She was always cheerful, but — underneath the sunny smile — I'm pretty sure she's a shrewd judge of character. I liked her, and she was a tremendous sounding board when I felt that no one else was listening. Without her support, I'm not sure that I'd have remained such a strong advocate for Kevin's safety. Due to her job, her involvement had to be limited, but she encouraged me — sometimes on a daily basis — to get help for Kevin.

Pippi was a downstairs neighbor and single

mom in her 20s. She was an on-again, off-again friend for Ann, and — during this same time period — Pippi made some poor life choices, herself. That turbulence was far more visible to our neighbors than what was going on in Kevin's apartment.

I was Kevin's neighbor. I'm happily married to Pete. When we lived next door to Kevin, Pete worked second shift at his office, so he witnessed some things that I didn't, and vice versa. Pete and I have three children. I write travel articles and books under a pen name.

The Story So Far

WARNING: If you haven't read the previous book about Kevin ("Momma, Don't Hit Me") — but intend to — this summary contains spoilers.

...

In October 2011, single mother Ann, her son Kevin, and Kevin's father (Joe) moved into the apartment next door to us in October 2011.

Initially, I liked Ann. She described herself as a full-time student working three jobs while raising Kevin. At the time, he was three years old.

Soon after they moved in, I began to hear Kevin screaming in his bedroom at night. It sounded like he was crying "Daddy, stop! Daddy, no!" over and over again, and I heard hitting noises. Since I liked Ann but Joe seemed sullen and distant, I assumed that Joe was the abuser.

I reported those incidents to both our landlord and apartment manager, but I wasn't ready to talk to the police until I was sure what was going on.

In the months that followed, I realized that Ann was the likely abuser. Joe seemed completely oblivious to what was going on in Kevin's bedroom.

I began calling the police every time I heard abuse in progress, next door.

Ann soon quit school, went through a string of jobs, and her behavior became increasingly erratic.

I filed more reports with the police. I called, emailed, and sent printed reports to New Hampshire's child protection office in the Department of Health and Human Services (DHHS).

I also talked with Joe, Joe's mother, and some mutual friends. I contacted other NH offices, and spent long hours with my minister, discussing Kevin's family problems and the shortage of community resources to deal with child abuse.

Joe had never married Ann, so he didn't have many options as a parent. Recently, Ann had charged Joe with domestic abuse. That made things worse for him. Joe was still in an anger management program, so he wasn't likely to get custody of Kevin.

Meanwhile, Ann got involved with drugs and prostitution. Late at night, even when Joe was at home (apparently a sound sleeper), it was like a revolving door at Ann's. A stream of men and women visited her, starting around 11 PM. They'd stay with Ann for 20 or 30 minutes or so, and then leave.

Then, a new tenant moved in. We nicknamed "Handshake King" (also called "HK" in my diary) because, when unfamiliar cars arrived in our apartment's parking lot, he'd shake hands with each driver, through the car window. Then, he'd pace around, go back to the car, and shake hands with the driver again. After that, the car would speed away.

Neighbors guessed Handshake King was a drug dealer or an undercover cop.

Handshake King seemed to be involved with both Ann and another neighbor, Pippi. Sharing "HK" with Pippi seemed to push Ann too far, and she responded badly.

She went back to prostitution. According to Joe's mother, that's how Ann supported her drug habit.

Soon, Ann's late-night abuse of Kevin became increasingly severe. Often, around 11 PM — and sometimes later — Kevin was in our building's hallway, unsupervised, dressed only in stained underpants and sometimes a shirt.

That was alarming because our neighbors included at least one registered sex offender, and our building had no lock on the front door.

I called the authorities during each lengthy bout of child abuse, but it never seemed to help. DHHS had too many cases to handle, and the police were frustrated by laws that required more evidence than I could give them.

As Ann's apartment lease approached its end, Joe moved out and took Kevin with him.

And, since it was election season, I compiled my diary entries as a Kindle book to share with people running for office. I hoped my book would highlight problems in New Hampshire's child protection system.

I thought the story was over.

About a week later, I discovered that Joe didn't have full custody, after all. He was sharing Kevin's care — in a rotating three-day/four-day split — with Ann.

So, Kevin was with Ann half the week, and — with Joe out of the house — had no protection from her impulsive and twisted style of parenting.

That's where this second part of the story begins.

The Diary Entries

Tuesday morning, October 2nd

After nearly a year of listening to abuse next door, it's almost *weird,* getting a full night's sleep.

Around two in the morning, it sounded like Ann had a temper tantrum and pushed over Kevin's dresser. In the silence that followed, I glanced at my clock and remembered that *Kevin is with Joe now.* I fell back asleep in minutes.

This morning, I felt amazingly refreshed. The past year has been exhausting, and I think my sleep was more interrupted than I'd realized.

I'll bounce back from this, after a few more nights' sleep.

Kevin's recovery won't be as swift, but I hope he gets the help he needs.

Today, I'm putting my blog entries together as a Kindle book. It's election season and this topic might attract campaign attention. Kevin's story could show that New Hampshire's laws need improvement.

Kevin is safe now, but I wish I'd been able to get help for him, sooner. Things need to change in this state.

Tuesday afternoon

I heard Ann go downstairs and apologize to Pippi, another neighbor.

They'd been at odds for months, since Pippi had embarrassed Ann. One sultry summer night, when Pippi knew Ann was listening, Pippi had asked one of Ann's boyfriends if he and Ann were a couple. The guy had laughed and replied, "No, we're just friends."

11

Ann hadn't expected that. She and Pippi had a loud argument a few days later, and ignored each other after that. For awhile, that boyfriend wasn't around much, either.

Today, Ann stood in the hall. Pippi wasn't letting her in.

Ann spoke loudly. "Listen, I just wanted to apologize for being a bitch lately."

"Umm... okay," Pippi replied.

"Yeah, I've been under a lot of stress, y'know?"

"Sure." Pippi didn't sound convinced.

"My whole life, I've never had time to myself, until now. First it was my parents, then Joe and Kevin. It's not right, y'know?"

Silence.

Then Ann laughed bitterly and said something about how hard it had been, having to be a mom to both Joe and Kevin.

Pippi — a single mom with boyfriend problems of her own — laughed. "Yeah. I know how that is."

Ann sighed and said, "Yeah, I guess you do. But, I wanted to say I'm sorry, and make sure that we're cool."

"Sure. We're cool."

So, Ann and Pippi are friends again.

That's pretty mature of Ann. Maybe it's a *good* sign.

Since then, Ann's apartment has been silent. I guess that's a good thing, too.

Later, I went to my mom's home for some empty glass jars. (She always has a few on hand.) We have a bunch of fruit flies in the kitchen and bathroom, and I don't know where they came from. I'm making fruit fly traps with the jars, putting a little vinegar, water, and sugar in them. The flies climb in, they drown, and the problem is solved.

Really, if that's all I have to worry about now,

life is *good*.

Another weird thing, now that next door is so quiet: I can hear Pippi's music, and her daughter stomping around, in the apartment below us. It's a little loud, but that's *normal* for apartment life.

Normal is good. I think I'm going to enjoy this.

Wednesday morning, October 3rd

I can't believe how much better I'm feeling. Today, I'm going to the library, to start researching my next book.

The days are cooler now. That also helps me sleep better. Last night was almost chilly. People are saying it'll be an early winter. I hope they're wrong. I want some nice, normal days for a while.

The past year has been brutal. I feel really selfish saying that, but the child abuse next door has taken a toll on all of us.

Mostly, it's going to take me awhile to get used to the silence. I'm so accustomed to Ann's abuse and Kevin's hyperactivity, it feels like something is missing now. I'm uneasy, and kind of looking for something to explain it. I know that's silly, but there it is.

Ann is on her own. She'll either figure things out or she won't. That can't be my issue.

Kevin is safe. Our lives are getting back to normal. That's all that matters.

Wednesday evening

Arrghh. As I was walking to my car, to go to the library, Joe was dropping off Kevin.

Ann was outside on her balcony, crouched in her usual gargoyle pose, smoking a cigarette. Only her cigarette stuck out from the front of her hoodie. She looked part gargoyle, part like the evil emperor in Star Wars. Just seeing her up there gave me the creeps. It's like I'm living next to the undead or something.

Of course, Kevin didn't want to go into the apartment building. Joe nudged Kevin, and he walked a couple of steps forward and stopped.

Joe nudged him again, and Kevin inched ahead a little more. He turned and looked up at his dad. Joe glanced around the parking lot. Was he seeing if he had an audience? I'm not sure. Then, Joe looked up at Ann and gave a big shrug.

Ann shouted down at Kevin, "Buddy, you'd better get your butt in here right now."

Joe put his hands on his hips, and looked grimly at Kevin.

Kevin tilted his head up and made a face at no one in particular. Then he ran into the building, making a "vroom" noise, and vanished up the stairs.

I drove away, feeling kind of uneasy. I didn't expect to see Kevin return to Ann. I thought that was over.

During the day, it was a struggle to focus on my work. Something was *wrong*. I could *feel* it.

When I got home tonight, my kids said that Kevin had been kicking his bedroom wall — off and on — for nearly an hour.

At some point, probably while we were having dinner, Denise — the woman with the red car — arrived.

Since then, everything has been pretty quiet, but I'm not happy about this. I thought Kevin was going to be in Joe's care from now on.

Thursday, October 4th

I thought Joe had taken Kevin to safety. After that, I thought Kevin would be protected by the court system.

I also thought I'd resume my normal life, never again hearing a screaming child being hit, day and night. I thought I'd never again see Kevin in the hallway in just his underpants, unsupervised, around midnight.

(Our building has no lock on the front door. Anyone — including the registered sex offender in the next building — could have walked in, scooped up Kevin, and left with him, unobserved.)

This morning, I called Maryann, the apartment manager. She said Joe couldn't get a babysitter for the rest of the week, so Ann was watching Kevin.

Maryann says she's as tired of this as I am. She said to call her if I hear anything bad going on. Then, she'll call Joe or his mother.

In the past hour, Kevin has escaped three times, maybe four.

He's been escaping like this in recent months: He runs out of the apartment and down the stairs, as fast as his little legs can take him. He pauses just outside the front door. I'm not sure he knows where to go for protection, once he gets away from Ann.

Usually, Kevin runs out in a shirt and underpants. Today, even though it's a chilly 60 degrees (F) out, he's just in stained underpants that look frayed around the waistband.

No shirt. No trousers. No shoes.

During Kevin's escapes today, Ann has been bellowing in the hallway, as usual. The "nice" voice she'd used with Pippi...? *Gone.*

Each time, Ann waits far too long before she goes after Kevin. It's as if she *wants* him to run away and not come back.

I called Maryann and left voicemail. She called back about 20 minutes later, but — by then — Kevin had grown tired of the game. Either that, or he was locked in his room. I can hear him shouting in there, angry, but I don't hear anything like abuse. It's just Kevin having a temper tantrum.

Thursday afternoon

I'm *stunned.* I never saw this coming.

Joe showed up, but that's not the part that astonished me.

I hardly recognized him. He had a smear of grease on his cheek. He hadn't shaved. He wore an olive green knit cap and black leather jacket.

All I could think was "Eminem meets Marlon Brando."

It's not that cold out. Joe looked like a thug.

He knocked on Ann's door for several minutes. No answer. Then, he pounded his fist on Ann's door. No one answered.

I glanced out the window. Denise's red car was in the parking lot. That meant Ann and Denise *had* to be around, somewhere.

I opened my door. "Joe, they're around here, somewhere. Just wait a few minutes."

Joe looked at me with barely concealed irritation. "Yeah, I just talked with Ann on the phone. They're out for a walk. They'll be right back."

I replied, "Oh, okay."

I'm *sure* I stared. I was kind of in shock. Joe looked so *different* from how he'd look during the past year. He seemed like a cat waiting for a mouse. He looked *ugly.* I wondered if I was seeing the *real* Joe now.

Joe glanced at me. It was barely a flicker. Then, he made an elaborate gesture, as if he was studying his fingernails. He glanced at me for another split-second. Then, as if talking to the wall on the other side of the hall — in a tone I

16

could only describe as surly – he muttered, "Yeah. Thank you."

After that, very deliberately, he went back to studying his fingernails.

My stomach lurched. I closed my door and went back inside. I sat down, hard, on my sofa. All I could think was, "Wow. I might have made a *terrible* mistake."

I heard Ann, Kevin, and Denise return, and I heard Joe's voice. The conversation was either low or in a normal tone of voice. I didn't listen. I was too busy trying to figure out why Joe looked so different from the guy who'd lived next door for the past year. Everything I thought was true about Kevin's home life...? It could be wrong. Really wrong.

About 10 minutes later, I couldn't ignore shouting in the hall. Ann snapped at Joe, saying something about not being a free babysitter for Joe's problems.

Joe said he didn't have time to be a full-time dad. If Ann didn't hold up her half of the deal, Joe would get full custody. Then Ann would have to pay him child support for sticking him with the kid.

I was kind of stunned. Mostly, I felt sorry for Kevin, hearing his parents argue over who'd be "stuck" with him.

The shouting stopped abruptly and Joe left with Kevin. I could see them walking towards Joe's car. Kevin's shoulders drooped and I could see his little fists clasped in front of his stomach. He looked like he'd lost everything.

Joe got into the car and lit up a cigarette, waiting for Kevin. I watched Joe's fingers tapping impatiently on the steering wheel while Kevin opened the door and climbed into the back seat.

Then, the tires squealed as Joe drove out of the

parking lot.

I keep thinking of the act Joe put on with Ann around July 4th... the whole "happy family" routine. I'm recalling how Joe didn't even blink when Maryann and I told him what was going on in Kevin's bedroom, at night.

I'm remembering how strange it's seemed. For the past year, Kevin's screams have been loud enough to disturb others in the building, not just me. (I could hear people hammering on the ceiling or the wall. Always, the following day, neighbors muttered about how noisy Kevin had been.) Could Joe *really* sleep through that, night after night?

One thing keeps coming back to me: Joe is still in court-ordered anger management treatment after a domestic violence conviction. Maryann had suggested it had just been one of Ann's tactics to make Joe look bad. What if it wasn't?

About a week ago, Maryann said Joe's mom wouldn't let Joe and Kevin move back in with them, even without Ann. Joe's mom had said, "They don't have a home here any more."

At the time, that seemed strange. What grandmother wouldn't welcome her only son and abused grandson into her home, to make sure they were safe?

Maybe Joe wasn't as innocent he'd been pretending. Perhaps he's been putting on a big act, all along. With shared custody, Joe is off the hook, financially. He doesn't have to pay child support. Maybe that was his main concern. He doesn't need my testimony now. He's getting what he wanted.

This is pretty hard to swallow. I'm completely disgusted. Not just with Joe, but with myself. I saw what I wanted to see. I feel like an idiot.

This is exactly why professionals like DHHS need to assess situations like this. I'm inexperienced in this, and it looks like I'm a gullible idiot, too.

Oh, I *know* that Ann has neglected Kevin. I've heard her threatened to hit and beat Kevin, and then I've heard the sound of hitting, followed by Kevin's cries.

Ann is abusive, but Joe could be just as bad... or worse. I might have been conned. There's no *nice* way to say that.

Either way, Ann is still living here and Kevin will be a part-time visitor.

I'm so frustrated, disgusted, and depressed, I can hardly see straight.

My husband and I are talking about moving. Out of all the immediate neighbors who lived here when Kevin and his family moved in a year ago, we're the only ones left.

This used to be a nice building in a nice apartment complex. I don't *want* to move. I just want *nice* neighbors again.

Friday, October 5th

Last night, I heard Ann crying. Her sobs echoed against her bathroom walls. I wanted to feel sorry for her but — even though she's just a kid, herself — I don't trust her.

My husband said I should ignore Ann. She's just putting on an act, to get sympathy. I knew he was right, but it still tugs at my heartstrings to hear anyone crying like that. Even Ann.

I looked out the window. Denise's red car was gone. That meant Ann was on her own.

A few minutes later, Mrs. Bernier — Ann's newest downstairs neighbor — was knocking on Ann's door.

"Are you okay, dear?" Mrs. Bernier is an older woman and she has a soft, sweet voice. I think she's a librarian.

"No, I'm not," Ann replied. "I can't do this. I need my own life."

"But you're a mother, dear."

"I didn't bargain for this. Everyone thinks I'm bad, and I'm not. They don't know what Joe is like. He didn't even marry me. I can't do this." Ann gulped, and started sobbing again.

"I'm sorry, but you'll have to. That's what mothers do."

"I should have put Kevin up for adoption when he was born. That's what my family wanted. Everything would have been different... *better.*"

"You don't really mean that," Mrs. Bernier insisted.

"I didn't even get to finish high school. *I want my life back.*"

Ann and Mrs. Bernier continued talking. Mrs. Bernier sounded patient and soothing. She kept telling Ann that she was a strong girl and she'd get through this.

After Mrs. Bernier left, everything was quiet for the rest of the night.

However, I had difficulty getting back to sleep. I was feeling sick to my stomach again, wondering how much Joe had been using me.

Oh, I had no doubt that Ann was mistreating Kevin and neglecting him. I'd witnessed that.

Now, I've seen another side of Joe. I keep trying to blot his surly expression out of my mind, but it's haunting me.

For most of a year, I'd felt so self-righteous. Ann was the villain. Kevin and Joe were the victims. I'd wanted to believe everything was that simple.

This morning — more than ever — I'm not so sure.

I keep going over everything that's happened in the past year. Sure, I knew Joe was putting on a big act in front of Ann. He didn't want her to know he was leaving and taking Kevin with him, as soon as the time was right.

Now, I wonder if Joe's act was much bigger... and worse. Maybe he was putting on an act in front of me and everyone else in this building.

All of this leaves a bitter taste in my mouth and a vicious knot in my stomach. *How could I be that naive?* I'm a mom, myself. I've been a Girl Scout camp director. I *know* that parents can lie, and do a pretty good job of it, sometimes.

How much of Joe's nice, subdued manner was just an act?

There's not much I can do, whatever the answer is. The police can't help. DHHS doesn't help. Kevin's grandparents stopped their friendly visits at least six months ago.

I don't understand this. It's like I'm the only one who cares, but I have my own family to take care of. Ever since Ann moved in, it's affected my family and me. That's not fair.

Right before lunch, I called Maryann. I told her that, unless she can assure me that things will change soon, we're giving our notice. I can't help Kevin, and this has cost me too many sleepless nights and anguished days. I thought this was over, last week. I've had enough.

Maryann said not to worry. The sheriff will be here next week to give Ann an eviction notice. This will be over, soon.

Friday afternoon

Late in the day, Joe dumped Kevin at the front door. He didn't even walk Kevin up the stairs. Joe just waited in his car for a few minutes, and then drove away quickly. I guess he figured that was good enough.

After that, Kevin escaped from Ann's apartment several times. He was in a plaid flannel shirt and soiled underwear. Thank heavens, it's a pretty warm day, but still... it's not okay.

Kevin got all the way down the stairs and out the front door, at least twice. Ann took longer and longer to go after him.

I dialed the office right away. Maryann said to call her next time it happens. She'll rush over and collect Kevin, and bring him to her office while she called the cops.

And, of course, Kevin didn't escape again.

Friday evening

Ann is returning to her old ways. Tonight, at least three men visited her, one every half hour or so.

Around 10:30 PM, Kevin threw toys at the wall for about three or four minutes, and did his running-in-circles routine. I heard him drop to the floor, probably exhausted. Then, about five minutes later, he started kicking the wall rhythmically.

I didn't hear anything like abuse. No hitting or crying. The kicking sounded like raindrops after awhile, and I drifted off to sleep.

Saturday, October 6th

Maryann visited Ann this morning. Apparently, other neighbors complained about Kevin being outside.

I'm glad they called Maryann, but really, why can't they call the police, too? I'm fed up with this. When I'm the only one calling the cops and filing reports, it looks like a vendetta. I'm not the only one witnessing Ann's parenting problems, so I shouldn't be the only one calling the police.

I keep hearing "I don't want to get involved," or "You do such a good job of explaining what's going on," like that's good enough. Arrgghhh! I hate this.

Later, Maryann called me. She'd told Kevin that he could visit her office if he ever needed help. Apparently, Kevin just stared at Maryann, as if he had no idea what she was saying.

Then, Maryann asked Ann why Kevin keeps getting outside, mostly undressed and by himself.

Ann promised to keep a closer watch on Kevin. She said he got out yesterday because she was still in her robe and couldn't follow him right away.

That was a total lie. Her door was open and she was just sitting on the sofa, texting on her phone.

Maryann reminded me that this won't go on for long. Apparently, Ann is planning to move close to Dartmouth College "to date better guys."

I laughed when Maryann told me that. I couldn't believe it. Really, is Ann hoping to snag a wealthy, Ivy League husband?

Then I remembered one of Ann's regular "gentleman callers." His shirt looked starched and crisp, his hair was well-trimmed, and he walked... well, like he came from money.

Early last month, I'd noticed his black Lexus gleaming in the sun when I'd go out to check the mail. And — unlike most of Ann's visitors — his car wasn't piled full of empty fast-food containers and other trash.

So, maybe that's the kind of guy she thinks she can charm. For his sake, I hope she's wrong.

Then, I realized two very good things about Ann moving to Hanover:

1. Ann has no car. That would make joint custody difficult. Joe won't drive Kevin all the way to Hanover, especially in winter. Route 89 is pretty well maintained, but still... it's a long

distance with a hyperactive kid in the car.

2. Few Dartmouth guys want a girlfriend (much less a wife) with a four-year-old child. So, that's *another* reason Ann might be interested in giving up custody of Kevin.

This could be good. I don't want to expect too much, but sometimes I just need a glimmer of optimism in all of this.

In other news, Pippi and the boyfriend have been arguing half the afternoon. When they finally stopped talking to each other, one of them turned the hip-hop music up, *loud.*

I feel like I'm living in an asylum. It's like we're the only normal people here. But, to them, maybe we look like the weirdos. I try to keep that in mind. Moving away from this would be a whole lot easier than hoping the neighbors will change.

Meanwhile, we still have fruit flies. Everything's covered up in my kitchen, so they have nothing to eat. I have no idea where they're coming from. Maybe the warmer weather — yesterday and today — caused them to multiply faster...?

I don't know why I'm so concerned about them. Maybe it's because they're a normal problem. I need more normal stuff in my life.

Saturday evening

Around dinner time, Kevin escaped from Ann's apartment again. I called Maryann but I reached voicemail. I didn't bother leaving a message.

Ann scooped up Kevin and brought him upstairs telling him he was a brat and a pain in her ass, and she ought to just let him run away. About an hour later, Ann and Kevin left with a couple of backpacks. Denise — the woman with the red car — picked them up in the parking lot.

So far, they haven't returned.

Monday, October 8th

Last night, the peace and quiet were *wonderful*.

Ann and Kevin returned near lunchtime, carrying an extra backpack. Her hair had been cut and styled. It was a uniform color, with discreet highlights gleaming in the sun.

Her clothes were much more upscale, too.

Kevin smiled and he swung his arms as he walked. He was even wearing shoes. I hoped it was a good sign.

Denise helped Ann carry groceries into the apartment. They were chatting and laughing as they walked, and Ann seemed genuinely interested in what Denise was saying. In fact, Ann looked relaxed in a *good* way.

Maybe Ann's Dartmouth plans are exactly what she needs. Perhaps, with Joe around, Ann just didn't see much happiness in her future.

I don't actually *dislike* Ann, only her out-of-control behavior. Maybe she's just immature. And maybe Joe's influence was bad and put too much of a strain on her. It's difficult to guess, but I'm hopeful that things are changing for the better.

Shortly before dinner time, Ann's prep-looking boyfriend showed up. As usual, he was well-dressed. He carried a leather backpack that still had an airlines tag on it.

Ann and Kevin were at the top of the stairs, greeting him as he walked in. Ann's voice sounded normal, not forced and definitely not deep, grating, or ugly. Even Kevin seemed chatty.

After dinner, Ann, Kevin and the boyfriend went out for a walk. Ann and the boyfriend held hands and looked like a relaxed, normal couple with a child.

I hope it lasts. It's not the happy ending I'd expected for this story, but — if Ann doesn't slide back into her old habits — this could be a very good life for Kevin.

Tuesday, October 9th

When I woke up this morning, the sun was shining, the morning was crisp with a hint of autumn, and I'd had another good night's sleep. Next door, everything had been quiet.

My family seemed more relaxed at breakfast. I was even getting ahead of the fruit flies. Well, either that or the colder weather was affecting them. Either way, I was happy.

Around noon, Ann, Kevin and the prep boyfriend went across the street to the park. The boyfriend was carrying a cooler. The day was still pretty chilly, even in the sun, but Ann and Kevin were well-dressed. They looked like a real family.

I was reminded of July 4th, when Ann and Joe tried to put on a "happy family" act. I also remembered Ann and Kevin on their balcony with HK, an apparent drug dealer who dated Ann for awhile. None of them seemed to connect like a normal family.

What a difference! *This* looked real.

A few minutes later, Pippi and her daughter joined them with their own cooler. Pippi's daughter and Kevin ran around, kicking the autumn leaves and laughing. Everyone seemed light-hearted and happy. Honestly, I've never seen Kevin act so *normal*.

I could see them from my kitchen window as I prepared lunch, and — for a little while — I thought everything might work out.

Maybe the real problem has been Joe. Perhaps

he got Ann to act as the "heavy," and be the disciplinarian with Kevin. Maybe Joe was behind the tension in their apartment, and — with him out — Ann might unwind and become a normal mom.

Well, that's what I *want* to believe, but my gut is telling me it's not that simple.

Tuesday afternoon

Bleh. Sometimes, I *hate* being right.

Around two this afternoon, things began to unravel.

First, I heard the rental guys pounding on Ann's apartment door again.

Every couple of months, the rental guys show up with their truck. Two of them knock at Ann's door and she makes excuses for her late rental payments. The way Ann explains it, it's always Joe's fault. He didn't get paid on time. He forgot to send the check. He'd blown the money on a night out with his buddies.

She always promises to take care of the bill later in the day or first thing in the morning.

The guys go away for a few days or a few weeks, and then they're back again, demanding money.

Today, the rental guys seemed frantic. Maybe they're just fed up with her lies and late payments. They knocked at Ann's door, more and more loudly, for about ten minutes. I'd think their hands would be swollen from pounding on her door. Nope, one of them just kept hitting the door with his fist.

Finally the noise stopped. One of the rental guys slid a note under Ann's door, and loudly announced that she'd better read it.

About 30 minutes later, Maryann was at Ann's door. Maryann was *not* happy. Apparently, the rental guys had gone to the apartment office.

Ann sighed and said to Maryann, "C'mon in."

Maryann replied, "I don't think so. We can talk right here." I think she wanted witnesses.

Maryann said — pretty loudly — that it's not her job to act as the go-between for Ann and bill collectors.

Then, Maryann said that it didn't look like Ann was packing to move, either.

Ann said, "I'm getting the rent together. I just need a few more days."

"That's not an option, Ann. We're not renewing your lease. I've already filed eviction papers."

Ann tried to argue with Maryann, but got nowhere. Maryann left, and Ann slammed the apartment door.

About a minute later, Ann returned to the door and slammed it about five more times, hard enough that the remote fell off the edge of our table, in front of the TV.

When Maryann got back to the office, she called me. She wants me to be very watchful, and call her if Ann does anything suspicious.

While I was on the phone with Maryann, I heard shouting next door, followed by the door slamming one more time.

I pulled back my curtain to look outside. The prep boyfriend was running down the sidewalk towards his car. His shirt was untucked and it wasn't even buttoned right. He was busy pushing things into his backpack.

He got into his shiny black Lexus and peeled out pretty quickly. When he paused at the stop sign at the end of our driveway, he was talking to himself and shaking his head.

I'll bet he was thinking, "Lucky escape."

Tuesday evening

Around 6 PM, Denise arrived in her red car and paused for a minute. Ann hopped in and the two of them drove off.

I hadn't heard a sound from Kevin all day. I assumed that Joe had picked up Kevin, and I hadn't noticed.

15 or 20 minutes later, Denise returned, alone. As she was climbing the stairs, I heard Kevin. Apparently, he'd been left alone, and he'd opened the door when he saw Denise arriving.

Wow. If I'd known Kevin was on his own again, I'd have called the cops. I *hate* missing opportunities to expose Ann's neglect.

Everything was quiet until around 10:30 PM. That's when Ann came stomping up the stairs, cursing loudly.

I heard her walk into her apartment and shout, "That son of a bitch fired me again!"

Then she slammed the door.

Minutes later, Denise scurried out of the apartment and drove away.

What a day. First it looked like everything was going to work out for Ann and Kevin, and then it spiraled — almost out of control — into a complete mess.

I hope Kevin is okay tonight. I'm keeping my phone by the bed, just in case.

Wednesday morning, October 10

Early this morning, I dashed to the grocery store for eggs. When I got home, Ann was in the parking lot with Kevin. They were getting out of Denise's red car. I didn't even know they'd gone out.

Ann's hair was pulled back and smooth. Her clothing looked clean and wrinkle-free. She wore a blazer, not a hoodie. Her sunglasses were big and shiny, and they looked new. She was carrying her backpack hooked on her elbow, as if it was a purse. I think she was trying to look like Paris Hilton, and doing a pretty good job of it.

I don't know where Denise has been taking Ann lately, or what they're doing, but Ann's appearance improves each time.

I wondered if Ann was going to try to get the prep boyfriend back again. After yesterday's events, good luck with that.

Kevin had barely stepped out of the red car when he started running. He ran around to the back of the building, and Ann followed.

Seconds later, Kevin returned to our front yard, running back an forth and shrieking. I was reminded of the movie, *The In-Laws,* and the "serpentine" scene. I couldn't help smiling.

Eventually, Ann caught up with Kevin. She yelled at him, "I'll make you take a shower." (Kevin hates taking a shower by himself. Everyone in the building can hear his protests. So, that's become one of Ann's most recent threats.)

Ann carried Kevin for a few feet, and then dropped him to the ground. When he stood up, she grabbed his hand, almost savagely and pulled him behind her. Kevin stumbled and tried to dig his heels in. Kevin did not want to go into our apartment building.

The good news is, Kevin was fully dressed. That's unusual. He even wore a little down vest. Maybe Ann and Kevin will keep some of their good routines from when the prep boyfriend was here.

However, though Kevin's clothes were nice, they were rumpled and his hair looked like... well, my mom would say it looked like it had been combed with an egg beater. In other words, it was sticking out at all angles. "Bed head," at its worst. His face looked like it needed a scrubbing, as well. So, maybe Ann's "shower" threat was more about cleanliness than discipline.

I walked past them, smiled, and said hello. Ann didn't seem to hear me, so I kept walking. Behind me, they made a lot of noise on the stairs.

Wednesday afternoon

About an hour before the kids were due home from school, Maryann called me.

She said, "Stay inside your apartment. Whatever happens, stay inside."

I asked, "Why? What's going on?"

"You'll see. Just stay away from your door. Don't even look out. Act like you're not home."

That's all she'd tell me. Of course, curiosity was driving me crazy.

About five minutes later, I heard heavy footsteps on the stairs. Then, I heard someone knock loudly on Ann's door.

"Miss Claire? It's the sheriff. Open your door."

Silence.

"Miss Claire? We know you're in there. Open the door."

Silence.

"This isn't helping, Miss Claire. We're here to serve you an eviction notice. I think you know that."

Silence.

Then, I heard the sound of tape, and — after a few seconds — heavy footsteps on the stairs again, followed by a barked order, "Miss Claire, I suggest you read that."

I looked out the window and saw three men in Sheriff's Department uniforms, walking back towards two cars.

Then, they drove away.

I looked out the security viewer in my front door. The sheriff had taped an eviction notice onto Ann's door.

It's not a discreet note that was left in an envelope. Nope. It's big and bold, taped along all four edges. Anyone who passes Ann's door can see that she hasn't paid her rent, and she's been ordered to move out.

Wow.

I called Maryann and told her what had happened. While I was on the phone, I heard Ann open the door. I looked through the security viewer, and I could see Kevin behind Ann. His eyes were as big as saucers.

Ann looked distraught.

She spent less than a second reading the notice on the door. She didn't touch it. Then, she slowly stepped back inside her apartment, closing the door carefully and quietly, as if she didn't want anyone to know she was there.

I went to another part of the apartment and told Maryann what was going on. She seemed relieved, and — once again — promised me that Ann would be gone, soon.

Wednesday evening

After a silent afternoon, I heard something rattling — loud — in Ann's bathroom. Our bathroom and hers share a wall, so everything on her side echoes in our bathroom, too.

Then I heard knocking, followed by Kevin pleading, "Mom, I need to poop."

Ann replied, "No. I'm in here."

"Please, Mom!"

"Go away, bud. I'm busy."

"I need to POOP!" Kevin shouted.

"Too bad, buddy. Suck it up. You can't come

in." Ann's words were a little slurred. I wondered if she was in the bathroom, drinking.

Kevin continued shouting. It sounded like he was kicking the door, too. Ann turned on the shower, full blast, probably to block the noise.

A few minutes later, I heard hammering in Kevin's bedroom. It sounded like Kevin had a *real* hammer again. I heard crunches like he was hitting the sheet rock, hard.

I panicked and called Maryann. I stood next to our bedroom wall, to be sure that Maryann could hear how loud the hammering was.

Maryann said Kevin could tear up the apartment as much as he liked. She wasn't going anywhere *near* Ann after the eviction notice. Maryann said to call the cops if it sounded like someone was getting hurt, or if Kevin broke through to our apartment.

Great. I'm sitting here, waiting for an enraged four-year old — armed with a hammer — to break into my apartment so he can use the toilet.

...

My husband and I talked about the problem, and he took the kids to the mall. I didn't even want to go into the corridor, and *somebody* had to stay here, to keep an eye on things.

I sat on our bed with my phone in hand, ready to dial 911, wondering how I ever got into this *ridiculous* situation.

The shower kept running. The hammering grew louder.

Then, I heard footsteps in the hallway. It was Mrs. Bernier again.

She knocked on Ann's door. I don't think Ann heard her over the noise of the shower.

Mrs. Bernier knocked louder and shouted, "Ann, open the door like a good girl."

Weirdly, Ann turned off the shower. The

hammering in Kevin's room stopped a few seconds later.

I heard Ann say, "C'mon in," but Mrs. Bernier said she'd rather stay in the hall. *Smart woman.*

They discussed Ann's eviction. Ann was back in "blame everyone else" mode. Joe hadn't paid the rent. Joe abandoned her. Maryann wasn't patient enough. And so on.

Basically, Ann had the idea that the eviction notice meant she was being kicked to the curb, immediately. Ann thought the sheriff could come in and change the locks if Ann so much as set *foot* outside the apartment.

Mrs. Bernier read the eviction notice, out loud. Apparently, Ann has weeks to move. Until then, she can come and go as she pleases.

Of course, I wasn't happy to hear that.

A few minutes later, after some words I couldn't hear, Mrs. Bernier went back downstairs, and Ann went back inside.

Everything seemed quiet after that.

Thursday, October 11th

Bleh. More kicking and more shouting, off and on, all night. Around midnight, I heard the familiar sound of Ann throwing Kevin's door open so hard, it hits the wall in back of it.

A few minutes later, I could hear Kevin screaming "Stop. Momma, STOP! I'll be good!"

I called the police. It took them nearly 20 minutes to get here, even though they're only about a block away from us. That never makes much sense to me, but it's normal when I call them.

As usual, Ann had an excuse for the noise when two officers arrived. Since the eviction notice was still on the door, she pointed to it and said, "Look at what I have to put up with. Joe didn't pay the rent, and he didn't even tell me about it."

The officers — including one named Phil, who lives in two buildings away — weren't as sympathetic this time. They went into the apartment without saying much. Then, I could hear their voices in Kevin's room.

They said nothing when they left Ann's apartment. Total silence. Nothing from them. Nothing from Ann, except a low, wavering, "Thanks." That's unusual. I think Ann knows she's losing ground.

About 10 minutes after the cops left, Ann slammed her front door three or four times and shouted, "Bitch!"

After that, I heard Kevin kicking the wall, rhythmically, but that's all.

Late Thursday morning

My husband took the kids to the school bus stop, and — despite how little sleep I'd gotten last night — I had a good morning catching up on laundry and the next chapter of my book.

Late this morning, Ann and Kevin returned home after errands or something. Once again, Denise dropped them off in the parking lot. I was outside, on my way back from the recycling bin, so I had a good view of what was going on.

As usual, Ann paid little attention to Kevin. She stood at the edge of the parking lot, reorganizing the grocery bags she was carrying. Then, she seemed to stare off into space, looking at nothing in particular. Wool-gathering, I guess. Perhaps Kevin was counting on it.

He bolted.

Even though Ann was just feet from Kevin, he got away. He ran across the lawn — a distance of about 20 or 30 feet — and straight into the street. He didn't even pause to look for traffic.

As I watched in horror, everything seemed to happen in slow motion.

I remember Ann putting her groceries down, and rearranging one bag so it wouldn't fall over. Then, she put her hands on her hips and shouted, "Get back here, buddy." It sounded like a half-hearted shout, like she didn't really mean it.

At the same time, a shiny black pickup truck was barreling down the hill towards Kevin, from the left. An old white Oldsmobile was approaching Kevin from the right.

Kevin paused for just a split second, and then kept running. I remember seeing his skinny little arms bent and swinging, and his fingers splayed as he ran.

Next, I heard a double squeal of brakes. The pickup truck missed Kevin by less than a foot. The Olds had more stopping distance, but it was still too close for comfort.

Kevin ran another 10 feet, into the driveway across the street. Then, he paused. I'm not sure if he knew where to go from there.

That's when Ann finally yelled at Kevin to stop. She walked about ten feet, stopped, and shouted at him again. She just stood there, with her hands on her hips. Finally, she crossed the street to get him.

The driver of the pickup truck was gesturing with his hands. The elderly man at the wheel of the Olds shook his head with a grimace on his face.

I understand a child running into the street. My kids did it when they were really little. It was terrifying, but they never got far enough to be in danger.

What I *don't* understand is why it took Ann that long to chase Kevin. If she'd acted quickly, she could have reached him before he got to the street.

I'm also baffled because I saw *no* relief on her face as she brought Kevin — squirming frantically in her arms — back to this side of the street.

If one of my kids had been that close to a terrible accident, I'd be one step away from a total meltdown, relieved that he'd survived okay. I'd also have thanked the two drivers for stopping so quickly to avoid tragedy.

Neither seemed to occur to Ann.

If Kevin were my child, I'd then read him the Riot Act. I didn't even see that reaction from Ann. She seemed annoyed, but only as much as she usually is when she's taking care of Kevin.

How can a mom be that slow to react, and show so little emotion? I'm not sure. Is this what drugs do to her? I'm clueless.

At that point, my pulse was still racing. I was horrified by what I'd seen... and I was too far away to have any chance of catching Kevin before he reached the street.

Denise hadn't even opened her car door. She just sat there, watching Ann and Kevin through the windshield.

I didn't want to run into Ann and Kevin in the hallway, so I turned around and walked over to the mailboxes, as if to check my mail.

When I returned to my apartment, I heard Kevin screaming, followed by some slapping noises. By the time I reached my phone to call the police, Ann's apartment was silent.

A few minutes later, Ann emerged. I could hear Kevin inside, kicking the apartment door and throwing himself against it, but he didn't try to open it.

After that, Ann and Denise made multiple trips between Denise's car and Ann's apartment. It looked like they were bringing in enough groceries to stock a bunker.

Does Ann *really* think she can stay here very long?

Later that afternoon

About 10 minutes after Denise left, two police officers showed up. I guess another neighbor had called about the truck incident.

Once again, Ann made it all about Joe. She said Kevin was out of control since Joe left. Listening her talk — as if she was lecturing the entire building — I remembered that she'd been studying psychology last autumn. Now, she was pulling out all kinds of pop phrases.

It was really annoying.

I was relieved when the police weren't impressed. One said Ann needed to be more watchful. The day could have ended in tragedy for everyone.

Ann agreed, and the cops left.

Thursday night

A little before midnight, I heard Kevin's door slam against the wall. I knew what would follow.

I heard Ann's "ugly" voice, bellowing something at Kevin. Then, I heard Kevin crying, "No, please, Momma! No! Stop! I'll be good!"

Ann yelled even louder. Between hits, Ann was telling Kevin that it was all his fault and Ann's life was ruined the day she got pregnant with him. She said he'd spoiled everything, and it was his fault that Joe left.

I snapped. I couldn't stand another minute of it. I dialed 911 and told the cops to get here right away.

This time, they did. In fact, they could hear the screams and thuds, all the way into the hall. I think everyone in the building could.

Ann was out of breath when she answered the door. It took a minute for her to compose herself, but — wow — she was pretty fast with a good line.

"I've been expecting you," Ann said. "Kevin is completely out of control tonight. Can you talk with him?"

The cops went into Ann's apartment and closed the door. I could hear an occasional low voice, but that's all.

About five minutes later, the cops were in the hallway, getting ready to leave. They said they'd have to file a report.

Ann said, "Good. Joe shouldn't have left like he did. This is all *his* fault."

I'm not sure if the police knew how to respond. They just said someone from DHHS would probably contact Ann, to follow up.

I went back to bed. I heard Ann's voice in Kevin's room, saying something in her "ugly" voice again. Then, she slammed his door shut.

Everything was silent for the rest of the night. I was pretty sure it was the calm before the storm.

Friday, October 12th

After yesterday's drama — and two visits from the police — I wanted things to be very quiet today. For most of the morning, everything was pretty much normal.

From downstairs, Pippi's music was loud. The boyfriend sure likes hip-hop. It's annoying, but it's still *normal* apartment noise. That's okay.

Then, late in the morning, I heard Kevin throwing toys against the wall.

Sure, I've heard that before, but this was different. It wasn't his usual rhythmic throwing. This was hurling the toys — bam, bam, bam — in rapid succession, and so loud, it's like he wanted to smash them.

Then, he started roaring. It sounded like complete rage. No words, just long, *loud* shouts... as loud as he could make them.

Seconds later, Kevin escaped again. Wearing just a pair of soiled underpants, he bolted down the stairs and out the front door. He stood at the edge of the parking lot, facing the building, and dancing.

The weather was chilly but I was housecleaning, so my sliding glass door was open. I could hear Kevin shouting, "Momma is a POOP! Momma is a TURD! Momma is MEAN!"

He was wide-eyed and laughing, and practically singing the words. It was kind of creepy. His eyes reminded me of that guy who shot people in the Colorado movie theater.

Kevin had definitely snapped.

I picked up the phone and called Maryann. She said, "I'll be right there."

Less than a minute later, she was crossing the lawn, her keys in one hand and her cellphone in the other, calling someone. But, while Maryann was heading this way, Ann dashed out and grabbed Kevin by the hand. With a cigarette hanging off her lip, she shouted at Maryann, "It's okay. I've got him."

Maryann paused and watched while Ann got Kevin into the building. Then, she walked back towards the office.

I went out to the hall, to see if Ann needed help with Kevin. Ann is strong, but — overnight — it's like she dropped 20 pounds. Once again, she looks like skin & bone.

I leaned over the railing to watch them climbing the stairs, and asked, "Can I help?"

Ann looked up at me, startled.

"Naw. I've got him." She continued walking slowly up the narrow stairs. I could see she was leading Kevin by the ear, and he was yowling in pain.

"Ann, that's not a good idea. It can damage his hearing."

Ann glanced up at me and her eyes narrowed. "Yeah, I'll tell you what else isn't a good idea, and that's getting in my face. Mind your own f___ing business."

She kept tugging on Kevin's ear, pulling him up the stairs.

I went back to my apartment and called Maryann. She said she'd call Joe's mother, who works at a local clinic. I'm not sure if Joe's mom is a nurse, but she'll know how dangerous this is.

Later that morning

About an hour later, close to noon, I heard another shout followed by running down the stairs. I figured Kevin was escaping again.

I looked out the window, and saw Joe's mom getting out of her car in the parking lot. Kevin threw his skinny little arms around her legs, and she bent down on one knee to hug him.

Ann shouted across the parking lot, "This is all your son's fault, y'know."

Joe's mom looked disgusted. I didn't hear what she said, but I saw her gesture towards the apartment building as she took Kevin's hand and led him inside.

Ann raced ahead of them and stood at her front door, waiting.

"If Joe would just grow up, I wouldn't have to deal with this sh__," Ann announced, when Kevin and his grandmother reached our floor.

"Let's discuss this inside," Joe's mom replied, a

little winded by the climb.

They went into Ann's apartment, and I went back to work on my book.

About 20 minutes later, I heard a really loud cracking noise. It sounded like a plastic ruler breaking, followed by someone running down stairs.

I heard Ann shout, "Great example, *Grandma.*" The sarcasm was pretty ugly.

I looked out the window and saw Joe's mom walking rapidly away from the building. She was shaking one hand as if it hurt, and looking at it. Her palm was bright, angry red.

The next thing I heard was Ann on her balcony, continuing to shout. "I'm calling the cops. You better stay the f__ away from my kid."

Joe's mom didn't reply. She just got into her car and drove away.

Wow. Did Joe's mom hit Kevin? I'm kind of shocked, but I can't say I'm totally surprised. There must be a reason why Joe thinks *some* hitting is okay, or he'd have removed Kevin from Ann's reach, a year ago. If Joe's mom hit him when he was growing up, that could explain a *lot* about Joe.

Bleh. There is one of those days when I can't *believe* how much Ann and Joe intrude into my daily life. I want them to move away. Or we will.

But, even as I'm saying that, I know that my main concern is Kevin's safety. I don't like him very much, but he's the product of his home. No kid deserves that kind of life. He should have parents — and grandparents — who love him and care about him.

This is another one of those days when I wonder where Ann's family is. I might have seen her mom and sister when she first moved in, but that was nearly a year ago. I know there's an aunt, but I'm not sure if I've ever seen her.

Now, I just want Ann out of my life, and I want to know that Kevin is safe. I don't think that's too much to ask.

Friday afternoon

If Ann actually called the cops — which I doubt — they either didn't show up or they were really quiet. I was working on my book, and the kids were watching TV, so I might have missed what was going on.

However, after thinking about what I heard and saw, I called Maryann again. I told her about Joe's mom and the red hand. Maryann said Joe's mom had already called her.

Apparently, Joe's mom said Ann was in the kitchen. Kevin and his grandmother in the living room. Kevin had hit himself, loudly, and then shouted that his *grandmother* had hit him.

Joe's mom said *this* is why she can't have Joe and Kevin move in with her. Kevin is a liar, and — for all Joe's mom knows — maybe he's been hitting himself all along.

Is that possible? I have no idea. None of it makes much sense. I don't know who to believe now. Ann is a bad parent, but is Joe any better? And what *did* happen today, with his mom and Kevin?

Seriously, I can't get more involved in this ridiculous, awful situation.

Maryann told me to keep an eye on Ann, and let the office know if Ann seems to be moving out.

Friday evening

After writing that, I went back to work. Despite today's distractions, I got a lot done on my current book.

Late in the day, Denise picked up Ann and Kevin. They came back with even more groceries, about an hour later.

Denise, sat outside for at least 20 minutes. She just seemed to be watching our building through her car window. Then she got out of her car with a small backpack, and went into Ann's apartment. She didn't look happy. Very odd.

I get the feeling that Ann is up to something, and I can't tell what it is. She makes me nervous. She must have ice water in her veins, and — when I look at her — I get the idea that the gears are always turning. She's always scheming something or other, and something *is* going on tonight... I just don't know what it is.

The only good news is, with Denise in the apartment, Kevin is less likely to be abused.

Saturday, October 13th

Around 1:25 this morning, Kevin was kicking the wall and shouting last night, but I heard Ann's voice only once and just for a minute.

About 20 minutes later, Kevin threw a series of toys against the wall.

After that, I could hear him humming and making car noises, like he was playing. So, I went back to sleep.

I'm not sure when Joe showed up, last night. I didn't hear anyone arrive before I went to bed.

Then, before breakfast, I heard Ann's apartment door slam. I felt like a really nosy neighbor, but I looked out the window anyway.

Joe was walking across the lawn wearing something like flannel pajamas. He was barefoot, as he often is. He sort of sauntered, carrying his shoes and wearing a big smile.

Minutes after that, Denise left, too. She was tugging at her blouse, and trying to smooth her hair. It's difficult not to assume yet another threesome, but I try not to think about that.

Everything was quiet for the rest of the morning. My husband took the kids to soccer and Scouts. I was able to work on my new book, and didn't even stop for lunch. It was a good day.

Sunday, October 14th

Ah-ha! *Now* I know what Ann was up to, yesterday. Denise was the bait, and Ann's plan worked.

This morning, Joe moved back in. And, it looks pretty permanent. He brought furniture with him.

Yep, my family and I came home from church, and there was Joe with his dad, unloading the pickup truck. I could barely believe this was going on.

Joe looked happy. His dad looked grim. Neither of them said hello in response to my greeting, so we just walked past them.

Later in the day, it looked like Joe took Ann to work. She's wearing yet another restaurant uniform. I thought she'd run out of job options. I was wrong.

After Joe got home, I ran into him in the hall. He seemed kind of distracted.

Kind of hating myself for saying it, I reminded Joe that I'll testify in court if he needs my help. I told him that I won't *lie* about anything, but I can testify that Ann isn't fit to take care of Kevin.

Joe just stared at me. He muttered, "Yeah. I guess so." Then, he kept walking.

I was kind of relieved. I'm still not sure what Joe's role is in all of this.

A month ago, I was sure Kevin belonged with

his dad. Now, I'm *not* so sure, but still... if Joe were to open up and be honest about what's going on, I might be able to help.

Anyway, about five minutes later, I saw Joe again. I needed something out of my car, and Joe was under the hood of his car, right next to mine. He glanced in my direction and it's like I wasn't even there. He seemed to look right through me.

I said hello, but Joe didn't even blink. He just turned his head and went back to whatever he was working on.

Very weird. I'm not sure if Joe is a good guy or a bad guy in all of this. He's probably smart to shrug off my offer of help. I'd be happy to tell a judge about Ann's parenting, but I'd also have to raise questions about Joe.

My conscience is clear. I'm still worried about Kevin, but there's only so much I can do. I've called the police and DHHS at least two dozen times. Probably a lot more. I've written reports, too.

The cops can't do anything unless they actually witness the abuse. DHHS doesn't return my calls. I feel like I exhausted those avenues, months ago. So, I'll keep brainstorming with my minister and following Maryann's advice, as well.

Everything was quiet for the rest of the day. I heard Ann return home from her job, and that's all.

Monday, October 15th

If Kevin woke up — or was woken up — last night, I didn't hear a sound from his room. I kept waking up all night, feeling uneasy in the silence. Joe's return worries me.

This morning, I called Maryann as soon as the office opened. My greatest fear is that everything will go back to the way it was for the past year. No eviction, and no help for Kevin.

Joe lost my trust when he was deliberately rude to me, right after he'd moved out.

Maryann said that Joe had moved in with friends, but — just last week — they decided they needed to move... without Joe.

When Ann offered to let him move back in, Joe grabbed the chance. She probably didn't even need Denise to help persuade him.

However, Maryann assured me that the eviction *will* go forward. It's being processed right now. She said she talked with Joe about taking his name off the lease, so his credit won't have the eviction (for non-payment of rent) on it, but he didn't seem interested.

So, Maryann isn't feeling very sympathetic towards Joe. If he and Kevin are still in the apartment when the sheriff evicts Ann, they'll all be thrown out.

Maryann said she may have to go to court but the eviction is going to happen... soon.

I was barely off the phone when Ann knocked at my door. Wow. That might be the second time, ever.

She asked if I could watch Kevin for her. Apparently, Joe took off this morning, and didn't say anything. Now, Ann needs a lift to work and someone to take care of Kevin while she's out.

I said no, because I'm already late with my current book. And, I'm uneasy having Kevin in my home, without a third party as a witness. I mean, what if he really *is* hitting himself and blaming others? I can't take that kind of risk.

Ann's face twisted for a second. I didn't know if I was seeing shock, rage, or what. She just said, "Fine."

She went downstairs and talked with Pippi.

About five minutes later, I saw Ann walking out to a rusted, green car. She climbed in, on the passenger side, and leaned over to kiss the guy driving the car. It wasn't a quick kiss.

Then, they drove off.

Ick. I can't *believe* the number of men Ann seems to get to do her bidding. Right now, she looks like a scarecrow, bordering on anorexia. Her skin seems too tight. She always looks anxious. And, she spends a lot of time on the balcony, in her gargoyle pose, smoking cigarettes.

She's meeting guys in the parking lot regularly. That had stopped for awhile, after Joe moved out. Now, she goes out to their cars, they drive off for 20 or 30 minutes, and she comes back, smiling, putting something into her pocket as she walks back towards our building.

I always like to think the best of people, but — with Ann — it's pretty difficult.

Meanwhile, I'm not sure why Pippi wasn't at work today, but it seems like she's Kevin's new babysitter.

On a positive note, my husband installed weatherstripping at our front door, mostly to keep smells out of our apartment. We're pretty sure our downstairs neighbor, Pippi, is smoking marijuana. Or maybe it's her boyfriend.

Either way, they try to mask the smell with perfumed candles. Combined, the stench in the hallway would make you gag.

Since adding the weatherstripping, we don't smell much, and — weirdly — the fruit fly population has decreased in our apartment. It's a mystery. I also can't *believe* I'm actually obsessing about *fruit flies* in this diary when so much is going on, next door, but — somehow — it seems connected.

Tuesday, October 16th

Late yesterday, Ann returned from work. I heard what sounded like Ann and Pippi arguing in the hall, but I was in the kitchen, getting a head start on tomorrow's dinner. The kids were watching TV, and my husband was playing online games. So, I didn't pay much attention to anything outside our door.

If Joe came home last night, I didn't hear him. After Ann's argument with Pippi, everything seemed quiet next door.

Despite that, I'm not sleeping well. I keep feeling like something is about to happen, but I think this is just a *Catch-22* thing. I'm on edge because I'm not sleeping, and then I'm not sleeping because I'm on edge.

I should probably talk with my doctor about this, but I'm pretty sure she'll recommend a sleep aid. The thing is, if something *really* bad happens next door, my husband is a sound sleeper and he might not wake up in time. I can't rely on the neighbors to call the cops, either.

Have I mentioned how much I hate this? Yeah. It's like that.

This morning, all *Hades* seemed to break loose when Ann brought Kevin to Pippi's door.

Pippi was the first to raise her voice, saying crisply, "I told you last night, I'm not a babysitter."

"Yeah, well I'm stuck with Kevin and I've got nowhere else to put him. If I don't show up for work today, I'll get fired."

Pippi replied, "Not my problem." Then, I heard her door slam.

After about three seconds of silence, Ann shouted, *"Real* helpful. Thanks a *lot.* I've got friends, y'know. You'd better be looking over your shoulder."

Then, I think Ann asked a few more neighbors to babysit Kevin.

Several minutes later, I saw Ann in the parking lot, texting on her phone.

About a dozen feet away, Kevin tried to get into a few cars, kicking several because they were locked. Then, he picked up a rock and hammered on the window of Pippi's car. Luckily, he didn't seem to do any damage. Ann ignored him.

After a few minutes, Ann was back inside, arguing with Pippi. It was a short, loud, ugly conversation. I couldn't hear the words over the noise of my dishwasher, and — frankly — I didn't care. They sounded like a couple of mean girls in a cat fight.

A door slammed so loudly, our door rattled. I peered through the security viewer in our door, and saw Ann half-dragging Kevin up the stairs. I could hear his toes hitting he stairs, *thump-thump-thump.* It seemed to take forever for them to reach our floor.

Then, Ann shoved Kevin ahead of her and slammed the door behind them.

About a minute later, Ann opened her door and slammed it about ten more times. Then, she opened the door again, shouted the C-word into the hall, and gave the door a final, deafening slam.

That's when the police arrived at Ann's door. I'm not sure if Pippi called them or someone else did. They *had* to have been in the building during Ann's last outburst.

Ann denied everything. She said she was upset because she just got fired, and it's all Pippi's fault.

Then, Pippi started shouting up the stairwell, saying that Ann had threatened her. Ann said Pippi was a hot mess and everyone knows she's a liar.

After about half a second of complete silence, it

seemed like everyone was talking at once. Finally, one of the cops said, "Enough! Either you work this out like adults, or we're taking at least one of you in."

After the brief silence that followed, I heard Pippi's door close, downstairs.

After that, the cops left, telling Ann that she'd better start acting like an adult or they'd be back and things wouldn't go well for her.

Ann didn't reply.

Then I heard Ann go into her bathroom, slam the door about five times, and turn on the shower, full blast.

The water ran for a little over an hour.

For the rest of the day, everything was quiet.

Tuesday evening

Around 7:15 PM, my cup of pens fell over and my desk chair drifted a few inches. Everything around me seemed to distort a little, like in a fun house mirror. It felt like a long, slow, dramatic roll. The noise was impressive. I'm not sure anyone could talk over it, easily. It sounded like a really massive truck on the road outside my window, or as if a train had jumped its tracks and made its way past my building.

Since I'd gone to college in California, I knew what it was right away: a mild earthquake. However, most of our neighbors had never felt one, so it was a pretty big deal.

When it stopped, I checked on the kids and then went out to our balcony. People were gathering in the parking lot, and several others were on their balconies, talking with their neighbors.

If Ann, Joe, or Kevin were next door, they made no sound at all. Maybe none of them were home?

I don't know. I went inside and we turned on the TV for news bulletins. For a few hours, I actually forgot about Ann and Kevin. It was kind of nice to have something distract me from the ongoing problems, next door.

Then, around 10 PM, one of my kids came out of her bedroom and said Kevin was crying again. My husband turned off the TV, and — sure enough — Ann was shouting and Kevin was wailing. About 30 seconds later, it sounded like Ann was hitting Kevin's head against the wall. *Thud-shout, thud-shout, thud-scream,* then *thud-whimper.*

My husband called 911. The police arrived in less than a minute. They must have been nearby.

Once again, the noise stopped as soon as the police pulled into the parking lot. Ann met them at the door, saying that she was glad they were there. She said Kevin was having one of his worst nightmares, ever. She said that Joe had taken off again, and she could use some help, calming Kevin.

The cops left about 15 minutes later. One of them stayed behind for a minute, talking to Ann in the hall. He said that this kind of behavior had to stop, now. He didn't elaborate, but his tone was stern. So, at least *some* of the police have figured out what's going on with Ann.

Everything was quiet after that.

How much worse does this have to get, before someone does something, or we pack up and move?

I feel like Ann's issues have, once again, taken over my life. She's becoming increasingly erratic. I can't even hope for Joe to take Kevin away from this misery. I don't trust Joe and I know that Ann is an unfit mother.

How long will this continue until the police or

DHHS or a family member rescues Kevin?

I hate this. It's wrong and unfair, and... *I hate this*.

Wednesday, October 17th

Everything was quiet after that, last night.

This morning, Kevin was definitely next door and back to his manic version of "normal." He's been running and jumping for the past couple of hours. I think he threw himself against the wall once or twice, shouting something about Power Rangers. He's slammed against the apartment door a few times, too.

We haven't seen Joe in several days. In the past, he'd visited Kevin at least *once* every couple of days. But, maybe he's been around and I just haven't noticed.

Thursday, October 18th

This morning, Maryann visited with a couple of the maintenance guys. They wanted to check every room for any damage from the earthquake.

The earthquake had seemed pretty dramatic at the time, but aside from a few things falling over, nothing major happened in our apartment. I guess some other units have cracks in the sheet rock or ceiling, but we're fine.

After the guys looked in every room and every closet, Maryann went across the hall.

Ann wouldn't let them in. She said her apartment was fine.

Maryann wasn't happy about that but she didn't press the issue.

"So, Miss Ann, when are you moving out?"

"When I'm damned good and ready," Ann snapped back.

"No, that's *not* how it works. The law gives you time to move, but that's all. The sheriff will throw you out, if you're still here when your grace period is over."

Ann changed tactics. "I'm going to get Joe to catch up on the rent. I'll have him bring you the check when he gets home from work."

Maryann wasn't buying it. "No, we've made this clear to you and Joe. We're not renewing your lease. That's not just because you stopped paying rent. It's a lot of other things, too."

"Yeah? Well, we'll see about that."

Ann slammed the door.

I heard Maryann say to one of the maintenance guys, "Did you see that? This is what I have to put up with. It's crazy."

After that, everything was quiet next door. I could hear Kevin playing in his room, and watching his TV later in the day.

As of dinner time, Joe still hasn't returned and it sounds like Ann has locked herself in the bathroom again. I'd like to take a shower, but there's no hot water and not much water pressure either. Ann turned on her shower over an hour ago, and it's still running. I can hear her coughing, like she has pneumonia or something. It's a nasty, hacking cough.

Kevin is jumping off the furniture in Ann's living room, and throwing himself against the front door. Then, it sounds like he's marching... stomping on the floor, *hard*. And then, I hear him jumping off the furniture again. I'm glad we don't live underneath Ann.

Friday, October 19th

Several times before going to bed last night, we heard loud footsteps outside our door. Ann's apartment door opened and closed several times. It wasn't the slam-slam-slam noise of Ann or Kevin having a meltdown. It was more like Ann was coming and going, or she had visitors who arrived and left, every half hour or so.

I know that at least *one* of the neighbors thinks Ann has turned to prostitution. I'm not ready to jump to that conclusion, but — given her history — it makes sense. I think she's been fired from every restaurant in the area, and at least two grocery stores. Without a car, she's running out of options.

So, she *has* to be getting money from somewhere. I don't think she can rely on Joe for support.

Around 11 PM, the traffic to Ann's apartment seemed to stop.

Then, around two in the morning, we were woken up. Someone was pounding on our front door and shouting.

My husband went out to see what was going on. It was Joe. He was drunk, leaning against our door, and trying to force his key into our lock. When it wouldn't fit, he pounded on our door and shouted some more. The words were so slurred, it was hard to figure out what he was saying.

We didn't open the door. My husband shouted at Joe to go across the hall and sleep it off.

From Joe's response, it sounded like he'd mixed up the apartments. He apologized over and over again, and finally stumbled across the hall.

It took him several minutes to open his door. He didn't close it behind him, and it sounded like he fell on the floor, a few feet inside the apartment. It's a good thing the floor has thick wall-to-wall carpeting.

After that, we didn't hear anything from that apartment. But, at least Joe is back again. I'm not sure if that's good news or not.

This morning, Joe left for work at the same time as usual, and he didn't look any different than other days. It made me wonder — once again — how often he's been drinking to blackout. That might explain why he didn't seem to know anything about his son screaming in the next room.

Meanwhile, as I was writing this, a different child in our building just escaped. It was Pippi's daughter. The little girl was halfway around the building — just feet from a street that's busy today — before Pippi caught up with her.

That's one of several bad habits she's learned from Kevin. She's also slamming doors and running and shrieking, like Kevin does.

It's no wonder that Pippi doesn't want to babysit Kevin again. He's already been a bad influence.

Today, Kevin has been on his best behavior. Though he opened and closed the apartment door a couple of times, he never once tried to escape.

Strangely, I never heard Ann's voice at all. Either she's deliberately keeping a low profile, she was asleep or indisposed, or... she wasn't there. In other words, Kevin might have been alone again.

I thought about knocking on the door, to be sure someone is with Kevin. On the other hand, he seems happier and — frankly — safer on his own.

I paced the floor for about ten minutes with the phone in my hand, listening carefully to the sounds next door. If Kevin was alone, *this* would give the police the excuse they need to remove Kevin from Ann's home.

On the other hand, if someone *was* with Kevin... I'd just reinforce the opinion that I'm a nosy neighbor, further weakening my credibility when I explain what we hear, next door.

I really hate being in this position. I hate Ann

for what shes' doing. I hate Joe for being irresponsible, at best. I hate the neighbors for not calling the cops and DHHS to report what I know they're hearing.

And, of course, as soon as I started dialing the desk at the police department, I heard Ann coughing in the bathroom.

I put the phone back in its stand, and came back to my desk to write this. I need to get back in focus, write more books, and get us the heck out of here.

Kevin shouldn't have to live with parents who don't care about him, and we shouldn't have to live next door to a problem we can't seem to fix.

Tuesday, October 23rd

The weekend was quiet. I think Ann and Kevin are somewhere else. We haven't seen or heard Joe since Friday morning, either.

The silence has been wonderful and I've slept well. This morning, the only noise I heard was from Pippi's apartment. Her daughter has been really loud since last Monday, when Kevin spent the day with her.

In fact, Pippi's little girl is probably more noisy than Kevin usually is. However, she's never screaming, "Momma, don't hit me!" or anything like that. As a parent, I can tune out normal kid noises. *Every* child is noisy. Some are louder than others. In an apartment building with several families, that's normal.

Still, I feel sorry for Pippi. First, her daughter has been mimicking Kevin's bad behavior. Then, Pippi's on-again, off-again boyfriend seemed to be MIA again.

I checked on Pippi a few minutes ago, when I heard her sobbing. She's okay. She just needs a good cry. The boyfriend had been bringing women home when Pippi was at work.

She'd come home from work early, to pick up a file she'd forgotten, and she caught him.

She's better off without him.

What a building. Really. I feel like I'm living in an old, cheesy nighttime drama, like *Melrose Place* or something... but more tawdry and with a hip-hop soundtrack.

That idea makes me chuckle. I mean, Pippi has the over-bleached 1980s hair. Some of the rust buckets in the parking lot are from that era, too.

If I couldn't find *some* humor in this, I'd be too depressed to get out of bed.

It's time for me to put the finishing touches on my current book, and send it to my editor. It's only a few days late. She'll be pretty happy that I'm getting better about my deadlines. Each book brings us closer to moving. I try to focus on that... and look for more ways to get help for Kevin. Even my minister has run out of ideas.

Tuesday afternoon

Ann and Kevin are back. I heard them arguing, shortly after the mail carrier delivered something that required Ann's signature. I'm hoping it was the next step in the eviction paperwork.

I saw Joe arrive around 3:30 PM, when I went out meet my kids at the bus stop.

He left a few minutes later, carrying a duffel bag. Kevin wasn't with him.

I've quit trying to make sense of this.

Then, at about 4:00 PM, a man in a rain parka and hat was knocking at Ann's door. She didn't answer. He knocked again, waited, and knocked once more. (Since it wasn't Joe, I didn't bother opening my door to say that Ann was at home.)

Finally, the man left, placing what looked like a TV remote against Ann's door.

I looked outside, but no car pulled out of the parking lot. In other words, he's probably a neighbor... but why would he leave a TV remote at Ann's door?

Very odd.

Shortly after that, Ann opened her door and — once again — Kevin raced to get out of the building.

Ann, not leaving the top floor, shouted down the stairway at Kevin. That's when I went to the living room, to see what was going on. If my child had a history of running into the street, I wouldn't let him get more than five feet away from me, until I was sure he wouldn't run off again.

Standing next to her apartment door, two floors above Kevin, Ann ordered him to come back upstairs because he "wasn't wearing any clothes."

Kevin refused. Ann continued shouting, and finally said, "I'm getting really tired of this, bud." Then she told him he'd have to take a shower if he didn't come upstairs, and he wouldn't like it.

Kevin said nothing.

Ann announced, more loudly, probably for the benefit of the neighbors, "You're not allowed out of the apartment without an adult."

Kevin continued to protest.

Finally, Ann shouted at him, "Fine. Stay down there. The cops are going to get you. I'll call them right now"

Kevin sighed loudly and began to climb the stairs, as Ann snapped, "C'mon, Kevin. Move it. March."

So, as ordered, Kevin began plodding heavily up the stairs.

"Kevin, I'm getting really tired of this. Quit stomping. I'm losing patience."

Kevin shouted back, as he continued to stomp, "March, march, march!"

And, with that, they both went back into Ann's apartment.

About 10 minutes later, Ann locked herself in the bathroom again. As usual, when Kevin said he needed to use the toilet, Ann told him to "suck it up, bud," and she turned on the shower, full blast.

This is getting ridiculous.

Right now, it sounds like Kevin is kicking his bedroom wall, hard. It's rhythmic and pounding, but quieter than a hammer and louder than punching the wall.

With each kick, the plastic outlet cover on our side is making crackling noises, like it's going to break.

I'll be really glad when Ann moves out. I hope the courts take away her custody rights.

That doesn't guarantee safety for Kevin, but it can't be worse than this.

Later in the afternoon

Wow. I just got back from shipping hard copy of my book to my editor. Two morbidly obese girls — about 13 or 14 — are dancing at the entrance to our parking lot. I've seen them before. One is a very pretty girl, and she walks a dog daily. I'm pretty sure both girls live in this complex.

Right now, they're taking turns using the pole supporting a decorative lamp, for very crude pole dancing. Do they *know* how vulgar it looks?

A group of boys, around ages 8 to 12, have gathered around them. One is carrying a beat-up, boombox-style radio, and the volume is high.

Seriously, we need to move. I gripe about our neighbors, but sometimes I get the idea that *we're* the misfits.

There was a time when the landlord sent notices to all parents. He said kids weren't allowed to play outside without adult supervision. That was over a year ago.

Now, we've got two girls pole dancing, the crowd of boys around them, loud music with lyrics I don't want my kids to hear, and — at the other end of the driveway — kids are throwing some kind of noisemakers on the pavement around a row of gas grills. I keep expecting one of the propane tanks to go up in flames.

I've called Maryann, and she's sending a maintenance guy to talk with the kids.

This is *insane*. We need to move.

Friday, October 26th

I've called the police *twice* this week. Maryann says that, if she has to go to court to get Ann out of the apartment, it will help if the judge sees lots of police calls. So, I call whenever I hear abuse or neglect, next door. Even if I know they won't get here in time — if they show up at all — I'm calling. Now that Maryann is getting involved, I want to do everything I can to help her.

Oh, I still *hate* it that I'm still one of the few neighbors calling the cops. *I* think it looks like I have a feud going with Ann, or something.

Maryann says no, the cops know *exactly* what's going on with Ann. They just need more opportunities to catch her in the act, and arrest her on something that's going to hold up in court.

Well, I'm all in favor of that. This has gone on far too long.

The thing is, since Joe left with Kevin at the start of this month, Kevin has been very different. He's only four years old, but I think he's realizing that his parents aren't very good people.

He still has outbursts. Some nights, I'm sure he's being abused, too.

On Wednesday afternoon, I heard Kevin retching in his bedroom, and Ann had locked herself in the bathroom with the shower on. My first call was to Maryann, who said that's neglect and I should call the cops. So, I did.

I called again on Wednesday night, when I heard Ann shouting at Kevin and hitting him.

Both times, Ann made up excuses when the police arrived.

In the past, that frustrated me. Now, I'm beginning to think that Maryann is right. The cops are being cheerful with Ann and acting as if they believe her stories.

But, as they leave the building, their body language suggests something else. I see shaking heads, and shrugged shoulders. Then, one of the officers stops near their car, and seems to be annoyed as he talks, usually with one hand resting on his holster and the other gesturing towards Ann's apartment.

After that, they drive away... slowly, as if they're expecting to be called back at any minute.

Until recently, it hadn't occurred to me that they're *only* nice to Ann so she keeps letting them into her apartment. One of these days (or nights), they're going to have the evidence they need. She still seems to see the police coming, but this can't continue. She'll slip up sometime, and I hope it's soon.

But, as I said, the cops aren't the only ones who've realized something's not right with Ann.

Lately, I've seen Kevin on his apartment balcony, watching the neighbors coming and going.

Sure, there are the unsupervised kids acting like tough guys, and girls... well, behaving badly.

However, Kevin also sees *other* families, including mine. He sees how we talk to each other. On the weekends, he sees dads outside, playing catch with their kids, even toddlers.

It's been a long time since Joe was outside with Kevin, being a normal dad.

Now, when I see Kevin on the balcony — and even in the hall — he's very quiet, as if he's thinking. Inside that little four-year-old body, I think he's figuring things out.

I think Ann has noticed this, too. When I see them together, Ann looks a little uneasy. There are moments when she pauses her bullying and I see a flicker of... I don't know... guilt? Fear? *Something* crosses her face, like she's having second thoughts.

Kevin is watching her. That's obvious. He's also talking more clearly. More often, I hear him shouting back at Ann, at least until she starts beating him.

I think he's figured out that his home life isn't normal, and nobody's going to save him from them. He has to save himself.

That's a pretty harsh reality for a four-year-old kid.

The smartest thing Ann could do is call DHHS and tell them what's *really* been going on. I'm increasingly certain that Joe isn't as innocent as he's pretended to be. I'm not sure he *should* have full, unsupervised custody.

I think Ann should move far away, too. When Kevin grows up and figures out what she did to him — even if Joe *is* partly responsible — Kevin is likely to be pretty angry. *That's* a confrontation Ann should worry about.

But, for now, I've had fewer reasons to call the police, despite Maryann's requests.

Kevin seems to be staying out of Ann's way. He's quieter.

Plus that, Ann spends a lot of each day in the bathroom with the door locked. I have no idea what Kevin is doing when he needs the toilet, but at least Ann isn't yelling at him and hitting him.

Also, I think Ann is trying to keep a low profile, if only to avoid eviction. Now — when she's not in the bathroom — she's trying to use her "nice" voice with Kevin. She's also taken him out for a walk. A couple of days ago, she let him run around while she sat on the lawn.

During those moments, I wonder if she's sorry for abusing Kevin, and trying to make it up to him. I have no idea. A *lot* of family counseling will be needed, to repair the damage she's done.

Anyway, I'll be alone this weekend. The kids are going camping with my husband. It's a Scouting event, and families are invited.

I love camping, but I'm staying home. I need to work. In the past year, I've missed two book deadlines. That's two too many.

With some luck, Ann will remain on her best behavior this weekend.

Saturday, October 27th

I should have gone on the camping trip. Well, maybe. I feel kind of selfish saying that.

Oh, I accomplished a lot yesterday evening. But then I heard three guys arrive at Ann's door. They turned the TV up, loud, and then... Ann left. She just walked out. I didn't hear her say goodbye to anyone, or say when she'd be back. She just walked out, without Kevin. She wasn't dressed for the cold weather... just a tube top, shorts, and flip flops, like it was the middle of summer.

I called Maryann about 20 minutes later, when it was clear that Ann wasn't coming back in any hurry.

Maryann called Joe. Apparently, he was watching a game at a neighbor's apartment, so he got here pretty quickly.

Joe tried to get the guys out of the apartment. All of them — including Joe — sounded pretty drunk. At some point, the police arrived and then Joe's parents showed up, followed by Ann.

The police took Ann's three friends out to the parking lot. Then, Joe's parents started lecturing Joe and Ann. The apartment door was still wide open. I think everyone in the building heard what was going on.

The next thing I knew, Ann was running down the stairs, shouting that she didn't have to put up with that kind of ignorance. I saw her cross the street, texting madly. Less than a minute later, a car pulled up and stopped, and Ann leaned over to talk to the driver.

After a couple of minutes, Ann got into the car and they drove away. It looked just like a hooker scene from a cheesy movie. But, for all I know, the driver was a friend, responding to her text message.

Joe, Kevin, and Joe's parents were still in the apartment. They still hadn't closed the front door. Both of Joe's parents were yelling at him, telling him to grow up and act like a man.

I could hear Kevin in his bedroom, sobbing inconsolably. Poor little kid. He deserves better.

I slept late this morning. I'm not as focused as I'd like to be, but I'm determined not to let Ann and Joe's problems disrupt my work.

Saturday afternoon

Ann came home, still wearing the tube top and shorts she'd left in. Her mascara was smeared under her eyes.

Joe rushed out of the apartment and challenged Ann before she even got to the apartment door.

He bellowed, "What the f___ do you think you're doing?"

All I could think was, "Wow, *that's* a pretty open-ended question. *I'd* like to know what Ann thinks she's doing, too." I *know* this situation isn't funny, but — sometimes — I can't *not* laugh at how ridiculous this is. It's the only alternative to feeling so frustrated I want to punch walls, myself.

Out in the hall, Joe seemed to tower over Ann, not just because he was standing on the landing above her, but because his arms were wide, gesturing wildly.

Through the security viewer in my door, I could see the color drain from Ann's already pasty-looking face. Then, her eyes narrowed and her jaw jutted out a little.

"I couldn't get a sitter, okay? And I didn't know where the f___ you were. You haven't been around since when... Monday? Tuesday? What the f___ was I supposed to do?"

I'm not sure if Joe had a hangover or what, but his retort was... well... fast and furious. "Quit f___ing making this about me all the time. You're his mother. You're not supposed to just walk out and leave him with a f___ing bunch of drunks."

Ann pushed past Joe, heading towards the apartment. Joe quickly threw his arms high over his head. It's like he knew I was watching, and wanted to be sure I saw that he didn't touch Ann. Or maybe he's just dramatic like that. I'm not sure that I care, one way or the other.

Ann rushed into the apartment and locked the deadbolt behind her.

Joe followed her, but I guess he'd left his keys in the apartment. He rattled the doorknob a few times, said something under his breath, and ran down the stairs, taking them two at a time.

I went back to my desk. I could hear the shower running, next door, but I think Ann really *was* taking a shower this time.

After that, Ann and Kevin were completely quiet.

Sunday, October 28th

When I came home from church, half a dozen neighbors were clustered around the apartment door, looking up at Ann's balcony.

Kevin was out there, by himself. It's pretty chilly today — high 40s (F), maybe — and he was in his underpants... and nothing else.

He was crying, and leaning over the balcony... a little *too* far over it.

My husband rushed our kids indoors. They didn't need to see this, and I knew it could end *very* badly. It's at least a 30 foot drop from Ann's balcony to the pavement below.

Digging through my purse for my phone, I asked one of the neighbors what was going on. She said she just got there, but it seemed like Kevin had been locked out on the balcony. Ann wasn't letting him in.

I was dialing Maryann's office when I heard her voice from behind me.

"Okay, what's up?"

Another neighbor replied. "It's that little boy again. I don't know how long he's been up there, but he started shouting about five minutes ago. He says he's been bad and his mother won't let him back into the apartment."

Maryann dialed the police, told them to get here, and then she shouted up at Kevin.

"Kevin, honey, where's your mom?"

Kevin looked like he was shivering. He sobbed and said something I couldn't understand.

Maryann tried again.

"Kevin, you need to go back inside."

Weirdly, Kevin decided it was time to climb *over the balcony.* I think he was planning to jump to the awning over our building's front door.

Maryann whispered, "Oh, my God." Then, shouting at Kevin, she said, "Kevin, honey, don't do that. Stand by the door and I'll get someone to let you in."

Thank heavens, Kevin paused and made eye contact with Maryann.

By then, about 20 people stood below Kevin, looking up at what was going on. The police ran past us, up the stairs to Ann's apartment.

Through the building's open front door, we could hear the police shouting Ann's name. It also sounded like they were trying to break down her door.

The rest of what happened was kind of a blur. I saw Ann and two policemen step onto the balcony. Ann seemed more horrified by the crowd below, than by the danger to Kevin. He was still straddling the balcony railing.

One of the officers scooped up Kevin. Another grabbed Ann by the arm and pulled her indoors.

The next thing I knew, the police were rushing Ann and Kevin to the waiting squad cars. Kevin was wrapped in a soiled blanket. Ann was in a bathrobe, stumbling, shouting, "You can't do this. I didn't *know* he was outside. He must have locked himself out. I didn't know..."

Less than a minute later, they were gone and the crowd started to break up.

Maryann started walking back to the office and shouted over her shoulder, "Let's hope they can at least charge her with neglect, this time."

I agreed, and went indoors.

About 20 minutes later, Maryann called me. Apparently, the police needed statements from anyone who'd seen Kevin try to get back inside. Either the neighbors didn't see him even *try* to open the door, or they just said they "didn't want to get involved."

According to the cops, the lock on the sliding glass door *was* loose. With jostling, the door wouldn't actually lock itself, but it would be difficult for a little kid to open.

In other words, the cops weren't sure charges would stick. If anything, *Maryann* and the landlord might be blamed for not maintaining the building.

Bleh! I give up.

Really, for the past year, Maryann and I have been trying to get the cops here in time to actually *see* how bad things are for Kevin.

They finally get here to see Kevin, in soiled underwear and nothing else, ready to leap from a third-floor balcony... and they *still* can't charge Ann with anything, to get Kevin out of her custody...?

I'm disgusted.

Apparently, Ann said she was in the shower. When she last saw Kevin, he was watching TV. She said she'd told him to get dressed, and she got into the shower, herself.

Unless there's a witness to give the police more to work with, Ann is *still* considered innocent. The cops have a long list of circumstantial evidence pointing at Ann being a bad parent, but even Kevin won't say she locked him out on the balcony. In fact, he doesn't want to talk to the police at all.

The police will file a report with DHHS, of course, but on DHHS's own website, it's clear that close to half of all reports are never even assessed.

And, after my first book was published, a politician explained that, due to privacy laws, no real oversight is possible. So, *no one knows* whether it's a DHHS budget issue, a management issue, or what.

That's not DHHS's fault, or anyone else's. It's the tangled legal system, and some *really* misguided applications of privacy laws. The whole thing needs to be overhauled. Kids like Kevin are falling through the cracks.

I hate this. I really, really *hate* this.

About two hours later, Ann and Kevin returned. Joe showed up later in the day. I have no idea where he was, when Kevin was on the balcony. I swear, neither of these parents are fit to take care of a child.

So, Joe and Ann shouted at each other and Kevin cried in his bedroom. After that, the TV was on in the living room, really loud.

Nothing changes. I'm so fed up with this, I can't see straight.

When my husband and kids returned from their camping trip — which sounded like wonderful fun for them — I told them I'm ready to start packing and move out of here.

My husband reminded me that we're probably weeks (or less) from Ann being evicted. Besides, it's going to be about six months before we've saved enough for a down payment on our own house.

It's silly for us to move now, but really, I wish we'd moved as soon as we knew Ann and Joe were bad neighbors.

And, even as I write that, I *know* I'm being selfish. Kevin is the real victim in all of this, and if today's events can't pry him loose of Ann's custody... I don't know what can.

I'm due for a good cry.

Tuesday, October 30th

If Joe, Ann and Kevin made any noise last night, I wouldn't have heard them.

News reporters are calling last night's storm "Frankenstorm." The wind howled, branches came down, and I guess a lot of people are without power. Portsmouth and the Isles of Shoals got it worse than we did. Our lights blinked a few times, but that's all, so I guess we're lucky.

I went out with a camera this morning, on foot, taking pictures of wet leaves coating a lot of roads, and trees that fell in the park across the street. About five huge pines came down, and one is still blocking the road. Two more crashed through the white picket fence separating the park from the nearby community center.

It's nearly stopped raining now, but — with the wind — I was soaked to the skin in about ten minutes. Worse, when I came home, Ann was running her shower again, so I couldn't get a hot shower myself. So, I've been sitting here at my desk, wrapped in my robe, going through my photos. Some of them are pretty dramatic.

Frankly, the devastation kind of echoes my mood. If the police can't charge Ann with anything, even after Sunday's near tragedy, I don't have a lot of hope for Kevin's safety.

Right now, it's still raw and windy outside. A lot of businesses are closed for the day. Some communities have postponed trick-or-treating until the weekend, when the power is sure to be back on. So far, our Halloween is still on schedule.

Tuesday afternoon

Things have taken a sudden turn for the

better... for us, anyway. I'm not so sure this is better for Kevin.

Ann and Joe have been loading his dad's truck with furniture. Right now, they're across the hall — with the door open — arguing about where the furniture is going to go. The truck is close to full, and there's still a whole lot of stuff still inside the apartment. Ann is saying something about a garage she has access to, for storage.

About 20 minutes ago, I actually had to go out to the hall and explain to them how to get a huge, junky, particle-board desk down the stairs. The were trying to get it around the corner, without turning it up on its end. The desk was already battle-scarred, and they'd knocked a piece out of one side, trying to navigate our narrow stairway.

My impulse was to say, "Just drop it off the balcony, and haul the pieces to the dumpster."

I understand that people hold onto cheap and shabby stuff when it's all they can afford, but still... *wow*.

I should *not* be critical. Hey, as long as Ann is moving out, I'm happy.

I'm sure Maryann will be relieved, too. She wasn't looking forward to a court hearing if Ann fought the eviction. Maryann knows what a skilled liar Ann is. We've seen her in action.

I hope the family is splitting up, and Kevin is going back to live with Joe. I still don't trust him, but after Sunday's events, he's better than Ann.

Well... maybe.

Wednesday, October 31st (Halloween)

When I went to bed last night, Ann and Joe were still making trips with Joe's dad's truck.

This morning, I was on our balcony, putting up the last of our Halloween lights, when Joe hauled away the last truckload of stuff.

The good news is: Joe took Kevin with him. The bad news: Ann is staying here.

There were no goodbyes this time. From the balcony, Ann shouted at Joe, "Fine. You want him? Take him and, this time, don't bring him back. I never wanted to have him in the first place."

I don't think Ann has an ounce of maternal feelings. The world evolves around Ann, as far as she's concerned. Everyone else is just a supporting actor.

From where I stood, it looked like Kevin was barely listening to his mom. He seemed more interested in the neighbor walking a cute little terrier, about 20 feet away from Kevin.

And, to be fair, I think Kevin is used to this kind of comment from Ann.

As Joe and Kevin drove off, I saw Kevin look back just once. His face was expressionless. There was no wave.

I *want* to feel relief, but my gut says this isn't over. I can't *stand* Ann, but I don't trust Joe very much, either.

Still, unless Ann has another meltdown, I can look forward to a good night's sleep tonight.

I wish I felt better about Kevin's future, but I went through this before, about a month ago. For me, this is like waiting for the other shoe to drop.

I hope I'm wrong.

Thursday, November 1st

I'm pretty sure Ann was out last night. I didn't hear a sound from her apartment until really late. And, even then, it might have been another neighbor.

As usual, we made a big deal out of Halloween. We decorated the balcony and our apartment

73

door. Our kids had painted a sheet with ghosts and creepy-looking trees, as a background for when we opened the door. And, we had really good candies this year — like real, full-size Reese's Cups and some glow-in-the-dark bracelets — so visitors were really happy.

My husband took our kids to the mall for trick-or-treating. I dressed up like a witch, and handed out candy and treats. We all had fun.

I think fewer than half of our neighbors actually have *anything* for trick-or-treaters. In most cases, I don't think they can afford it. The longer we live here, the more new tenants seem to be on welfare or... well, I don't know how they're supporting themselves. They sit outside and smoke a lot, during the day.

They seem nice enough. They're just going through difficulties. A lot of people have, since 2008.

Anyway, it's hard not to look back over the past year. Exactly one year ago, in 2011, I sat at my front door and chatted with Ann, who'd just moved in. Joe took Kevin trick-or-treating, because Ann had homework for her psychology class at the local community college.

I remember Ann, dragging a recliner across her living room, to keep the apartment door propped open. She sat in it with a bucket of candy at her feet, and wrote her term paper on her laptop.

I'd asked her if she'd already gotten the Internet hooked up in her apartment. She laughed as if I'd told a joke, and said, "Hey, all I need is unsecured wi-fi."

That night, everyone seemed to know Ann by name, and like her. She said she was working three jobs — while going to school, full-time and raising Kevin — and most people knew her from the local grocery store. Ann decorated cakes in their baking department.

I was impressed. Ann seemed bright and interesting, and sounded as if she cared deeply for children. She said really nice things about each child's costume. She complimented the parents if the costumes were homemade, and so on.

The only thing that had set off alarms for me was when I referred to her husband. Ann snapped, "He's not my husband. He's just my *partner.*"

I figured they must have had a fight, and she was still angry. Young couples have problems. The first couple of years my husband and I were together... we definitely had some rocky moments.

In general, I liked Ann and I was relieved to have a nice neighbor for a change.

The previous tenants had been heavy drinkers, and the wife didn't like me.

Maybe it's because, when that couple first moved in, they'd knocked on our door with a religious tract. (They were in a church that requires all members to knock on people's doors, weekly, looking for new converts.) I'd declined the magazine she tried to hand me, and explained that we're happy with the church we attend.

If I'd accepted the magazine, I was sure she'd be back to talk to me about it. I didn't want to build up her hopes. I did my best to be polite, but I could tell she was offended.

After that, she acted like I'd declared war on her. Or vice versa. She used to go into their bathroom when she heard one of us in our shower, and she'd flush the toilet repeatedly, cackling each time.

Anyone in the shower would first get the shivers when the water was reduced to a near trickle, and then get scalded when the pressure came back before the cold water did. I made sure my kids took their showers when the neighbors weren't at home.

I told Ann about that, and we'd both laughed. She said not to worry, she was a responsible tenant. We'd probably hardly know she and her family were next door.

Later that night, I told my husband about our nice new neighbor. He'd shrugged and said her voice was like fingernails on a chalkboard. He didn't like Ann, on sight, but — since I thought so highly of her — he said he'd give her another chance.

That seems *forever* ago. My husband was right. It just took me awhile to figure out that Ann, not Joe, was the most likely abuser when I heard Kevin screaming.

Still, I don't really care if Ann stays next door or not. Kevin has been my biggest concern. I don't *like* Ann, but as long as she's quiet and I don't have to deal with her boyfriends... I don't really care one way or the other.

I mean, for all I know, the next neighbors could be even worse.

Thursday afternoon

Wow. A friend just visited Ann. The two stood in the hall so Ann could make sure the *entire building* heard the conversation. Well, that's how it seemed.

After saying a lot of not-nice things about Maryann, Maryann's husband, and Joe's mother, Ann said that she's trying to move to a neighboring town this weekend.

Mostly, she's fretting over the $2k TV (she mentioned the price several times) from the local rental shop, and if the TV will fit in Denise's car without breaking.

I called Maryann and let her know what was

going on. I was pretty sure that, it being the first of the month, Maryann thought Joe, Kevin, and Ann were moving out today, at the very latest.

Maryann wasn't happy to hear that Ann is still in the apartment, but she's sure that this may be concluded, soon. Maryann joked that we can all stand on the balcony and sing the goodbye song as Ann drives away.

About an hour after that, someone from the power company showed up at Ann's door, demanding payment. Ann tried her usual line about her husband forgetting to pay the bill, and Ann would make sure it brought it in, in the morning.

That didn't work.

Then, Ann said her son was with his dad and he'd be home soon. She plead for an extension of the deadline.

That didn't work, either.

Ann sobbed dramatically, but the bill collector was a woman with a good, thick skin. She turned on her heel and went downstairs saying, "Call my supervisor if you want. My orders are to collect the money in cash, or turn the power off."

About five minutes later, Ann's apartment was completely silent. No TV. No hum of the refrigerator. Not a sound.

Friday, November 2nd

When I was getting ready to go to bed last night, I heard Ann in her bathroom, crying.

Even Mrs. Bernier didn't come upstairs to see what was going on.

Then, the crying stopped abruptly. I'm not sure if was all an act, trying to get sympathy, or what.

And, y'know what...? I don't even care. I hate myself for being so insensitive, but there it is. I'm worn down. I'm tired of being woken up in the middle of the night. I'm tired of calling Maryann, the police, and DHHS.

I wonder how many of our neighbors have been through this before, and *that's* why they didn't call the police when Kevin was screaming. Maybe they knew it wouldn't do much good.

I've turned into such a cynic. I hate this.

Early afternoon

Well, *that* happened a lot sooner than I'd expected.

Joe showed up with Kevin at about 10 this morning. Ann wouldn't let either of them into the apartment.

So, they had their conversation in the hall. Joe said his babysitter was sick and he needed Ann to watch Kevin, just for today.

Ann said Kevin wasn't her problem any more. Besides, she was pulling a double-shift at the restaurant, so she couldn't take him.

I think Ann has stopped trying to sound like a good mom. Today, it seemed like she was talking about someone else's child, not her own.

Joe put his arm around Kevin's shoulder and led him back downstairs.

I went to the window to see what happened. Joe was leading the way back to his car, and then Kevin just sort of stopped. He glanced over his shoulder, looking up at Ann's apartment. I don't think he saw me. He seemed pretty focused on Ann's balcony, which I can't see from my apartment.

Maybe she was on the balcony, or at the sliding glass door where he could see her. I don't know.

Then, Kevin sat down on one of the stairs near the curb. He put his little head in his hands, and I could see his shoulders shaking with sobs.

I felt so sorry for him. He's only four years old. *No* child should feel unwanted and unloved. It's just not fair.

Joe came back, put his hands on his hips, and told Kevin to get up.

Kevin slowly dragged himself up, as if he was a tired old man. Then, he followed Joe to the car. Kevin was dragging his toes with each step, clearly unhappy.

Joe was already in the car with the engine running. He didn't lean over to open the car door, or anything. Kevin climbed into the car, and they drove off.

This *isn't* the happy ending I'd wanted for Kevin. In fact, the past month isn't what I'd expected, at all.

I'd really hoped for *more* from Joe, as Kevin's dad.

Joe probably hoped for more, too. When Ann got pregnant in high school, Joe gave up college and a sports career. Whatever Joe expected from life, it sure wasn't this.

He went straight from being a high school sports hero with offers from football teams, to working at the local factory to support Ann and Kevin.

I'm trying to understand Joe and feel sympathetic. But, every time, I run straight into the memory of him in the knit cap and leather jacket, being a real *jerk*.

I don't know *what's* an act with Joe. Maybe most of it is. He knows I'm watching him and so is Maryann, and *she* calls his mom. So, Joe has a lot of reasons to put on an act around us.

I *want* to like him. I want to think he's the best parent for Kevin. But... I don't know. Something seems *wrong*.

Even today, I'm not seeing a tender, caring dad. The emotions don't reach Joe's face. His body language in the parking lot... it doesn't seem right.

I'm probably being too critical. I'm really, *really* tired of this drama.

Friday, November 9th

Ann's power is back on. I have *no* idea how she managed it.

For the past week, Ann has been quiet. Mostly, she's stayed at home. A week ago, when she said she had a double shift and couldn't take care of Kevin...? She never left the apartment.

I'm pretty sure she has no job at all. Well, nothing legal, anyway.

Most nights, it's a revolving door at her apartment, with men coming and going every hour or so, starting around 10 PM. Some mornings, the hall smells like someone dumped a bottle of cheap whiskey on the carpet.

I'm uneasy about that. Ours isn't the only apartment with children, and if Ann's turned to prostitution, that's not acceptable. We have some shady looking neighbors, and at least one registered sex offender in the complex, but this is different. It's next door, just feet away from us.

Yesterday, I finally snapped. When I took my kids to the school bus stop, there was a stinky pool of vomit just outside Ann's door.

I was furious.

I called Maryann. She sent someone over right away to clean up. I asked about the eviction. Maryann said she'd called the sheriff's office on Monday. They said they couldn't find the papers.

So, Maryann had to go back and file the paperwork all over again. Despite that, she's pretty sure we're just days from Ann being thrown out, at the very most.

I hope so. I really can't stand this much longer. I keep thinking this is about to be over... and then it isn't. My nerves are shot.

My husband reminds me that Ann might be thrown out today. It's been 30 days since the eviction notice was served. Ann's time is up.

Friday afternoon

I'm still hoping to see the sheriff here by the end of the day, but something else happened that threw me for a loop.

Around 4 PM, Joe arrived with Kevin. This time, Joe was in his knit cap and black, leather-ish jacket again. (On closer examination, I'm pretty sure it's vinyl, not leather.)

Though it's close to freezing outside, Kevin was in a tee shirt and trousers. No jacket. His hair was jutting out, this way and that, and he had a dried-on mustache, like he'd been drinking chocolate milk... but not recently.

Joe was carrying Kevin's backpack plus two big green trash bags.

Joe dumped it all at Ann's door, and — through the security viewer in our door — I saw Ann open the door.

Joe said, "Take him. I can't do this."

For the first time in months, I saw genuine disbelief on Ann's face.

"What do you mean, 'take him'? I don't want him back. He's *your* son. *You* deal with it."

Joe's voice grew softer, but his words were still crystal clear.

"I can't do this. I'm sh– as a parent. I can't seem to keep a sitter. You've got to take him."

Ann's mask seemed back in place as she said, "No. Can't do it. I have to leave for work in an hour. Take him to your parents. He's not my problem any more."

Joe said, "I'll pay you. Tell me what you want."

"What do I want...?" Ann voice grew louder with each word. "I want both of you out of my life. Just leave me alone. That's what I want. I put up with your sh__ for too f____ing long. Either leave or I'm calling the cops."

Joe gave Kevin a shove towards Ann.

Joe said, "I told you. I can't do this." And, with that, Joe turned and ran down the stairs.

Kevin just stood there. His little shoulders seemed to quiver a little, and then sag. Even Ann looked shocked.

She turned and ran into her apartment, and then I could hear her shouting from her balcony. "You can't do this. Give him to your parents, or I'll have Child Services take him away."

Joe shouted back, "It's up to you. I've got people waiting for me."

Ann shouted, "Yeah. That's *real* mature."

Then, she slammed the sliding door *so* hard, the screen door popped out of its track and went flying over the balcony, clattering on the pavement below.

After that, Ann slammed her front door, repeatedly. Kevin must have been inside. His backpack and the garbage bags weren't in the hall, either.

With *slam-slam-slam* going on in the background, I called Maryann. Apparently, Joe's mom said Joe was having troubles. She and her husband were staying out of it.

So, Maryann wasn't completely surprised that Joe is abandoning Kevin.

Maryann said I should call the cops if I heard anything weird at all. Maryann said the sheriff's office promised to evict Ann before Thanksgiving.

That's all Maryann could guarantee. She asked me to sit tight, and keep a close watch on Ann and Kevin.

Maryann reminded me that she's sleeping with the phone by her bed, and I should call her if anything happens, whether I call the cops or not.

I felt powerless. I'm exhausted. It's like the past year — and especially the past month — has drained all the energy out of me. Heck, we've ordered take-out food nearly every night this past week. My book...? It's at a complete halt. My husband is picking up the slack with the kids, bless him, but still... *this isn't right.*

I'm sorry, but Maryann doesn't have to live with this. I don't know why I'm angry with *her,* because she's probably doing all she can, but still... hearing "Call me if anything happens" and "This will be over, soon," isn't enough any more.

I feel like I've been carrying most of the weight of this for too long. I'm not even related to Kevin, for heaven's sake. It's just my bad luck that they moved in next to me.

Feeling completely fed up, I walked to the police station and told them what's going on. A really *nice* officer talked with me through the glass. She said that — for law enforcement to step in — they need evidence of a crime. They're watching Ann carefully. With cases like this, it's just a matter of time.

Meanwhile, she recommended DHHS. She said they can do more than the police can, with cases like this.

I nearly lost it, right there in the police station. I told her that, even when I sent DHHS a long, day-by-day diary of the abuse, they didn't respond.

She shrugged and said, "They have a lot on their plate. I wish I could say this is the worse case I've heard about. It's not. Trust me, you don't want to know how bad it gets, and we *still* can't do anything."

Then, the officer said something that surprised me. She said there have been thefts at the condos in back of our building. She said an officer is watching our building at night. So, if I hear anything and call 911, they can get to Kevin in a matter of seconds.

She said I could just go out on my balcony and shout. That might be the fastest way to get help.

At first, I felt relieved, knowing help was that close at hand.

But, by the time I got home, the idea of burglars... that worries me. I *knew* this wasn't as nice a place as it was when we'd moved in, but actual *crime*...? That's new and I *really* don't like it.

Tomorrow, I'm taking the kids to my mom's house. She'll be happy to take care of them until this ugly mess is over.

Wednesday, November 14th

Ann's apartment has been completely quiet, except for Saturday night when Ann had a shouting match with Kevin over Spaghetti-Os. It ended with Kevin being sent to his room.

About three minutes later, it sounded like he threw a dish at his wall. Then, everything was silent for the rest of the night.

Meanwhile, a marked police car has been parked across the street starting around dinner, each night. I think that's scared away Ann's nightly visitors.

Also, Maryann said the police haven't caught the burglar, but she *thinks* the mini crime wave may be over.

So, our kids are back here for now. As long as

Ann doesn't have weird people visiting her at night, again, I'm okay with this.

Ann has been going out to check the mail, several times a day. That's the only time we clearly hear Kevin. It's like he waits for Ann to go out, each time.

Then, I hear him jumping and shouting and making kid noises. Usually, he's pretending something about Power Rangers, his favorite heroes. However, it sounds like they're defending him from his mom.

Kevin puts on his deep voice and shouts, "You'd better stop hitting him, right now!" Then he says in his deep, Power Ranger voice, "Don't worry, Kevin, *we'll* protect you."

As soon as Ann returns, everything is silent again.

The rest of the time, it sounds like Ann is either watching TV or she's locked herself in the bathroom.

As long as Kevin isn't being abused, I'm counting my blessings... and taking this one day at a time, but my nerves are pretty much shot.

Wednesday afternoon

The rental guys were back. These two men were even bigger than usual. Their truck didn't have the rental shop logo on it, either.

Ann let them in, but she left the apartment door open and loudly sent Kevin to his room.

First, they took away two chairs and Ann's laptop computer. She didn't seem to care about the chairs, but she didn't want to give up the laptop.

Still, she was smart enough to hand it over, when one of them spotted it in the dining room.

Then the guys came back and asked Ann where the TV is. At first, she refused to tell them. Then she said Joe had taken it.

I *know* the TV is somewhere in Ann's apartment. Last time I saw the TV through the open door, it was propped up on an overflowing laundry basket.

The guys said they'd be back if Ann doesn't turn over the TV, soon. They warned Ann that it's an expensive TV. In New Hampshire, stealing it is grand theft.

Ann just said, "Yeah? Well, I'll look for it." Her voice wavered a little. I think she was pretty nervous about what the guys might do.

Then they left. I breathed a sigh of relief. Those were big, *scary* guys. I'm wondering how many places Ann has rented stuff from, and what's going through her head.

About 15 minutes later, I heard Ann watching TV again. It sounded like a *Lifetime* movie or something.

It's way too easy to get sucked into Ann's real-life soap opera. Really, I just want this over.

Thursday, November 15th

Kevin was kicking the wall for a while last night. Then, around 2:40 this morning, I heard Ann shouting in Kevin's room, and he was shouting back.

After that, I heard Ann hitting him, so I called the police. In about a minute and a half, they were in the hall, listening. I'm guessing they were already in our parking lot. That made me feel better.

Of course, everything turned quiet as soon as they got inside the building. The police rapped gently on Ann's door, and she opened it almost immediately. She said the noise was just Kevin having a nightmare again. She also said he'd fallen

86

off the sofa and hit his head on a toy.

Then, she started talking about Joe and how he'd "dumped the kid" on her.

The female officer backed away and said, "Ma'am, that has nothing to do with us. We're just here to be sure everything's okay in your home."

Ann kept rambling on, accusing Joe of all kinds of things, including abuse.

The male officer cut in and asked, "Is your husband in the apartment now?"

Ann said no, and he's not her husband, he's her ex-boyfriend. Emphasis on "ex."

The officer replied, "Well, you can file a report at the station tomorrow, if you want to. This has nothing to do with us."

Ann snapped, "Yeah, well, you come fast enough when that bitch next door calls you, but you can't help me? What kind of sh__ is that? I have rights, too, you know."

The officer said, "Ma'am, unless there's a problem in your home right now, there's nothing we can do for you. File a report at the station tomorrow."

Ann continued talking as the officers went down the stairs and back to their car. Frankly, she was barely making sense. It was just a string of complaints about her former boss, Joe, Maryann, Maryann's husband, and me.

I think Ann is kind of losing it.

Anyway...

Denise was back this morning. She hasn't been around in weeks. I'd been wondering if she was more Joe's friend than Ann's.

But, today she picked up Ann and Kevin, who went out looking surprisingly well-rested and well-dressed. I haven't seen them that fixed up since the prep boyfriend was around.

It's so rare that Ann puts this much work into

her appearance and Kevin's... well, I'm reminded of movies featuring con artists. Right now, I wonder what Ann is up to.

Thursday afternoon

The three of them — Denise, Ann, and Kevin — came back about a few hours later. Apparently, they'd been shopping. It took them four trips to bring all the groceries in.

Seriously, my jaw dropped when I saw them hauling in bags and bags of food, boxes of wine, beer, and *huge* bags of chips. Lots of bags of frozen food, like chicken nuggets, too.

Doesn't Ann realize she's about to be evicted? Apparently not. Or, this is denial on a *huge* scale.

Mostly, I'm wondering how she could afford all that food. I don't think food stamps cover beer and boxed wine. I'm betting she got all fixed up this morning to get money out of someone. I don't know who... but I don't really care, either.

During one of Ann's trips from the car to the apartment, I heard Mrs. Bernier open her door.

"Aren't you moving, dear?"

Ann snickered. "No, I'm not going anywhere. I've got a friend at the sheriff's office. He's taking care of everything."

Silence followed for several seconds. I think Ann was standing outside Mrs. Bernier's door, waiting for the reaction.

Mrs. Bernier's voice sounded thin and vague when she finally said, "Well... um... that certainly is a *lot* of food."

Ann just laughed and came upstairs. Denise and Kevin followed, with the final load of groceries.

So, *that* might explain what happened to the "missing" eviction papers, a couple of weeks ago.

One of Ann's friends probably misfiled them on purpose, or even shredded them.

Later in the afternoon

Ann and Denise and Kevin went back out again. This time, Kevin wasn't wearing a jacket or any shoes. It's pretty cold weather for that.

I heard Ann and Kevin return. About an hour later, Denise was back, with a duffel bag.

I have *no* idea what's going on.

I'm spending far too much time writing in this diary, and not enough on my book. This is like a really bad, suspense movie. I can't seem to look away until I know how it's all going to end.

Monday, November 19th

Denise spent the weekend. I have no idea what's going on. Is she moving in?

She left early this morning, but didn't take the duffel bag with her.

Later this morning, a man from the power company was here. Ann's check had bounced, so — yet again — her apartment has no power. I'm wondering what she's going to do about all that food she brought home last week. A lot of it was frozen food.

Or, maybe Ann will pull a few strings and get the power turned back on again.

For now, Ann's apartment is silent. I could hear her yelling at Kevin in another part of the apartment. Then, I heard him in his room, kicking the wall.

After that, a door slammed. I wasn't sure if it was Ann, throwing Kevin's door open, or what.

It sounded like she hit Kevin a few times. Kevin shouted back, "Momma, you'd better watch out.

89

I'm going to come into your room when *you're* asleep, and you'll be sorry."

Clearly, he watches too much TV, but he's also starting to defend himself.

If I was Ann, I'd be pretty worried about what Kevin will do when he grows up. If he goes for revenge then, that's an ugly crime waiting to happen.

I *want* to feel sorry for Ann, and the sorry situation she's in, but I can't.

Mostly, I'm less worried about Kevin now. He's getting older in a hurry. And, he's learning to stand up for himself. I'm not hearing a *healthy* reaction to Ann's abuse, but at least he's scaring her enough that she mostly leaves him alone.

Monday afternoon

Maryann just called. The sheriff will be here at some point between 11 and 3 tomorrow. Ann and Kevin (and anyone else) will have to leave. They'll be changing the locks on Ann's door, too.

Maryann said that the eviction paperwork had been sent to some office, not to her, and that office put it in a file instead of contacting her. So, Maryann had to walk the whole thing through, yet again, this morning.

The good news is: The sheriff wants to take the rest of Thanksgiving week off, so he's rushing all the evictions through, tomorrow.

Maryann asked us not to say anything about this, inside our apartment or anywhere that Ann might hear us. Maryann is trying to prevent Ann from preparing a scene. Maryann also asked us to stay off our balcony. She said to keep the curtains closed, and stay out of the hallway (except as absolutely necessary), to avoid confrontations. And, if Ann isn't there when the sheriff arrives, I'm to call the police if there's a scene when Ann *does* show up and tries to get into the (locked) apartment.

In general, we're not to have any contact with Miss Ann, as Maryann calls her.

Maryann had some not-nice things to say about Ann. I can tell that Maryann is nervous about this. She's pretty sure the eviction will involve yelling and accusations, if not a physical fight.

We're *not* looking forward to Ann's reaction, but Maryann says the police will do their best to arrive quickly if there are problems.

Maryann said this is just one of several evictions, this month, but it's the only really ugly one.

Meanwhile, Maryann called her friend at the rental shop to tell him what's going on. As soon as Ann is out the door, the rental guys — the legitimate ones — will be picking up what's rightfully theirs.

I told Maryann about the other rental guys. She said Ann's regular TV had been taken away last month, so she didn't know anything about the second one.

I get the idea that Maryann is just as tired of Ann as we are. She seems even *more* frustrated with Joe, but that's probably because she knows his mom.

Maryann said that she *still* couldn't get Joe to take his name off the lease, so Joe is going to have the eviction on his rental history, on file at the police department, at the sheriff's office, and on his credit report.

She says that a year ago, her *gut feeling* was not to rent to Ann and Joe. Now, she's wishing she'd paid more attention to that.

Tuesday, November 20th

I'm not sure what's going on. Here's the email I sent to Maryann, as soon as I got up.

Hi,
Just so you know:
At about 2:45 this morning, two guys arrived at Ann's apartment and she left with one of them. She left the other one with Kevin.
At about 4:30 this morning, Ann returned. We saw a car (not necessarily related) drive away a few minutes later... but neither one of us was paying close attention, so we don't know
how many people are still in the apartment. (The heavy clomping of feet on the stairs woke me up at 4:30, and my husband Pete was already up, working on a computer.)
Ann is definitely in the apartment, unless she tiptoed out quietly. But, one or more guys might still be there, as well.
So, as of right now (8:15 AM)... well, I wouldn't want Erik or any of the maintenance staff arriving before the sheriff gets here. Ann is probably alone, but it's not worth taking any chances.
Shannon

This was Maryann's immediate reply:

Good Morning,
Thank you for the update and they will not be going over without the sheriff. They will be over soon.
Maryann

Later

At about 9:30 AM, the sheriff arrived. He was

by himself. That surprised me. I figured he'd bring some deputies or assistants or something.

I looked out the window and saw Erik (Maryann's husband) and two maintenance guys standing out in the parking lot, looking up at Ann's apartment.

The sheriff knocked on Ann's door. She didn't answer.

He knocked louder, waited, and then shouted, "Miss Claire, open the door or I'll be forced to have it opened."

Ann said, through the closed door, "I'm getting dressed. You'll have to wait."

"I'll give you two minutes to open this door, Miss Claire, or I'll have the manager open it for you."

Total silence followed. I'm pretty sure *everyone* in the building had turned off their TVs and music, to listen to the eviction.

I felt like I was in an Alfred Hitchcock movie or something. Suddenly, the *tick-tick-tick* of our bathroom clock seemed like the loudest thing in the building.

Then, the sheriff's walkie-talkie squealed. I was so startled, I probably I jumped about a foot into the air.

The sheriff answered it, but I couldn't understand a word that was said to him.

When the conversation was over, he was silent for a couple of seconds. Then I heard a deep sigh, probably from the sheriff.

"I have an emergency, Miss Claire. When I get back, you'd better be out of the apartment for good."

And, with that, he dashed down the stairs, out the door, and peeled out in his car with the siren on.

He didn't return.

After that, there were no sounds from Ann's apartment. Not from Ann and not from Kevin.

I don't know whether to be worried or not. I don't know how desperate and depressed she is.

Wednesday, November 21st

Maryann called me a little after 8 AM. She sounded almost giddy.

"I told you Ann would be out by Thanksgiving, didn't I! Well, the sheriff is on his way over, and I'm sending two maintenance guys with him to open the door if Ann won't come out on her own."

This time, the hall seemed filled with men. I saw the sheriff plus two other guys in tan uniforms. Maryann's husband and two more men were on the stairs, just a few feet away.

The sheriff told Ann to open the door. This time she did, right away. Everything seemed very civilized.

One of the maintenance guys used a doorstop to keep the apartment door open. Then, all of the men filed into Ann's apartment.

The sheriff told Ann to leave the apartment.

She said she had things to pack up, but she could be out this afternoon.

He told her she had 20 minutes to get herself and her son out of the apartment, or she'd be forcibly removed.

Ann objected, saying she wasn't leaving without her stuff. Erik, Maryann's husband, told her she'd have a week to come back for her stuff, as long as she came with a police escort.

That seemed okay to Ann. She went into another room to get ready.

Meanwhile, Kevin was in the living room, in a wrinkled shirt and soiled underpants. I could see that through the security viewer in my door. His clothes must have been pretty bad.

Kevin wanted to talk with the sheriff. Kevin was very interested in the man's gun, and kept asking questions about it, and if the sheriff had ever killed anyone.

The sheriff kept telling Kevin that he needed to get dressed, because he was going to have to go outside soon.

It was like Kevin didn't hear him. He started running in circles around the living room, and then jumping off the sofa, over and over again, talking at the sheriff and the other men.

I have *no* idea what Ann was doing, but she came back to the living room with a pile of her clothes — still on hangers — draped over her arm, and she was piling food into her backpack.

She shoved Kevin's backpack at him and barked, "Get dressed, buddy, and put what you need in this. We're going out."

Kevin looked at the backpack, confused, and went back to jumping off the sofa. Ann left the room again. Maryann's husband tried to guide Kevin towards the bedroom.

About two minutes later, Kevin emerged wearing the same shirt, and a pair of stained trousers. He had a pair of mismatched sneakers in his hands, and his backpack looked empty.

Ann returned to the living room. She barely looked at Kevin, but simply brushed past him. He followed her out the door, and — clearly confused — walked slowly down the stairs.

I heard her shout, "C'mon, Kevin, move your *butt!*"

Kevin joined Ann out in the parking lot. She took his hand and they walked towards the convenience store about a block away.

I opened my door. Maryann's husband was in the hall. He looked at me, shrugged and seemed kind of disgusted. Then, he told the maintenance guys to check for any appliances left on, and be sure the apartment was secure.

I saw the sheriff walking around Ann's living room, studying everything. He went into the dining room, and then I closed my door.

About five minutes later, Maryann's husband knocked on my door.

He said, "I've changed the lock, and we've taped the door. If you see Ann or Joe, or if anyone tries to get into the apartment, call the police first and then us."

Then he warned me, "If you even *think* you hear something in the apartment, call us right away and *we'll* check it out. I don't trust her. She might get someone to break in and get her stuff, for her. She'll be arrested for trespassing if she tries to come back without a police escort."

I didn't know what to say. Was this really *over?*

The whole thing had happened so quickly, I was still in shock. After the failed eviction yesterday, I'd almost given up hope that Ann would *ever* leave. It seemed like the cards were always stacked in her favor.

Now, I can barely write this. I'm stunned. It's like the guys showed up, and Ann flew around gathering stuff. 20 minutes later — which seemed like just a few minutes, but also seemed like an *eternity* — the whole thing was over.

I've never seen a forced eviction before. I hope I never witness one again.

I *know* I should be worried about Kevin and where Ann has taken him. He didn't even have matching shoes on, when he left.

I just feel relief... sort of.

Mostly, I'm in a daze.

Monday, November 26th

Early this morning, Maryann was at Ann's door, unlocking it for the rental guys. I opened my door when I heard the noise, to be sure everything was okay.

Maryann laughed and said, "Don't worry. I'm just letting the guys in to collect their stuff. Want to see what she left behind?"

I hate how eager I was. I feel like I've become *such* a busybody, but still... I'd glimpsed inside Ann's apartment several times. Now, I wanted to see Kevin's room. If I understood the floor plan and where his furniture was, his noises might make more sense.

Inside Ann's apartment, the first thing that struck me was the smell. You know how people talk about the smell of rotting food, or vomit, or human waste? Ann's apartment smelled like all of them. I couldn't even describe the stench. I put my hand over my nose and mouth, trying to filter the air through my fingers. Maryann handed me a tissue. She was using one over her nose and mouth, too.

Then, Maryann started choking. She opened the sliding glass door to the balcony, to get some air in. That helped, but not enough. It was still disgusting. I figured that Ann must have left food on the kitchen counter, and it had rotted.

Next, I noticed the fruit flies. There were dense swarms of them, like something out of a nature film. When Maryann opened the balcony door, I thought they'd fly outside. Nope. They headed into the hallway, towards my apartment.

I ran across the hall and closed my door, and then went back to Ann's. So *that's* why I've been fighting fruit flies for the past couple of months.

Going back into Ann's, the first thing I noticed was the step on the right. It looked like Ann's hallway — to the bathroom and bedrooms — was elevated about five or six inches.

My hallway isn't elevated like that. *Very* odd. I was about to ask Maryann about it when I realized what I was looking at.

It was layers and layers of stiff, compacted, dirty clothes. Now and then, I saw part of a used diaper, mostly yellow but there were some flattened feces in the mix, too.

How long ago had Kevin been in diapers? In the past several months, I'd only seen him in underpants. Did he still sleep in diapers, or what?

I saw towels with what looked like vomit, too. Some of them were moldy, so it was hard to tell.

One of the rental guys walked over to the hallway, and picked up what looked like an adult's rugby shirt. As he lifted it, the shirt was as stiff as a board, and seemed attached to a pair of boxer shorts. More clothes came up with it, like some surreal daisy chain.

The rental guy dropped the shirt like it was on fire, and then he laughed. I'm not sure what he thought was so funny. I was horrified.

The thing is, the hall is about 15 feet long, and I saw no break in the filthy mass. There had to be at least 200 different pieces of clothing, diapers, and towels, at least five layers deep.

From there, I went to the dining area, mostly to get out of the way of the guys taking a torn and stained cloth sofa out the door. I figured they'd take it to the dumpster. There was *no way* to salvage it.

"Throwing that out?"

One of the guys grimaced and said, "No, it goes back to the shop. The boss will want pictures. We'll sue her."

I sighed and said, "Good luck with that."

Then, I noticed the animal cages in the dining

room. I was glad they looked too small to hold Kevin, because — at that point — I could only think the *worst* of Ann and Joe.

Seriously, Joe *had* been part of this. There's *no way* this amount of filth built up over the last couple of weeks, since Joe's last stay here.

At first glance, the kitchen — which opens to the dining area — seemed to have dark linoleum counters. A shiny new dishwasher gleamed, in contrast. (I was envious. My own dishwasher dated back to the 1990s and maybe earlier, and it didn't work very well.)

By then, I was getting used to the swarming fruit flies, and even the odor. Around the kitchen, it smelled like rotting cabbage and coffee. At least it wasn't human waste.

Then I realized that the counters weren't dark brown. They were thick with what I guessed was spilled food and coffee stains.

Maryann followed me, silently. She took her door key and scraped a line across a few inches of the kitchen counter. The groove was between 1/4 and 1/2 inch. Underneath, I could see the same white counter tops that we have in our apartment.

Maryann said, "That's disgusting." I nodded in agreement. There are things you can't find words for. The state of Ann's apartment... that's one of them.

Mostly, the kitchen counters and floor had piles of beer cans, probably a hundred cigarette butts, some take-out food containers, and about two dozen pizza boxes.

Maryann opened the refrigerator, and closed it almost immediately. The additional smell of sour milk and rotting food... I had to get out of there.

The hallway wasn't as thick with fruit flies as it had been, and the air was far better than inside Ann's apartment.

I took some deep breaths and went back in, because I *really* wanted to see Kevin's bedroom.

After everything else, I *thought* I was ready for the worst.

I wasn't.

The first thing I saw looked like lots of white and clear yellow plastic things, all over Kevin's floor. At first, I thought they were part of a really huge construction kit of some kind. You couldn't walk in the room without first kicking a few of them aside.

I reached down to pick one of them up. It was a yellow-orange plastic prescription bottle. As I glanced around the room I realized they were *all* drug store containers. Most seemed to be over-the-counter bottles of pain killers, sleeping pills, and allergy pills. I saw a few inhalers, and — mostly peeking out from under Kevin's bed — what looked like empty bottles of cough medicine.

I looked at the prescription bottle in my hand. The name on the label wasn't Ann's or Joe's. Maybe it was Denise's? I never knew her real name. The bottle had contained diet pills. That might have explained why Ann went from muffin to too skinny, and back again, regularly. Where I could see prescription labels, I saw "alprazolam" (Xanax) and something with codeine.

It was like standing in a dumpster from a hospital or pharmacy. *What were these doing in Kevin's room?* I'm still not sure.

The closer I looked, the more I could see paper plates and Styrofoam bowls between the bottles and the occasional toy. Many of the dishes were coated with a mottled green. It looked like dark moss and something like little twigs.

I realized it was rotting food and crushed cigarette butts.

My stomach lurched. A child had slept in here.

Less than a week ago, Kevin been playing in the middle of empty pharmacy bottles, rotting food, soiled diapers, and — the closer I looked — a fairly thick layer of cigarette butts, underneath everything else.

Kevin's bed was where I expected it, along an exterior wall. It had no sheet on it, just a soiled pillow without a case, a torn sheet, and a comforter wedged between the bed and the wall.

The mattress was soiled. I saw three areas of smeared feces, and then I spotted a couple of similar smears on the walls. I'm guessing *that's* what Kevin did when Ann wouldn't let him use the toilet.

As I suspected, Kevin's dresser was on its side. I'd heard something tip over the first time Joe moved out. I guess nobody picked it back up in the weeks that followed.

A few feet away, I saw a Winnie the Pooh lamp on its side. The lampshade was cracked and stained.

That's when I lost it. I just couldn't help myself. When I was a kid, I had a lamp a lot like that, in my bedroom... but *my* pretty, pink bedroom hadn't looked *anything* like this.

I burst into tears.

Maryann put her arm around my shoulders and agreed, "It's pretty bad. I've seen a lot, but I've never seen anything like this, either."

I turned and left the bedroom. On my way back to the living room, I glimpsed inside Ann's bedroom. Weirdly, her floor was mostly clean.

I'd seen enough. I was on my way to the door, when one of the rental guys shouted from the bathroom, "Hey guys, you have *got* to see this."

I peered around the corner of the door frame. I didn't want to get too close.

The rental guy was pointing at the counter by

the bathroom sink.

There, lined up in a tidy little row, were about 20 used tampons. Some were maroon, and others were dark brown. Their white strings hung neatly over the side of the counter. And, at an angle — just inches away — there was a child's toothbrush with dirty gray bristles.

I put my hand to my mouth, ran back to my apartment, and threw up.

I have never seen *anything* like it. It was like something out of a horror movie. In fact, if you saw it in a movie, you'd laugh and think, "Wow, they went crazy with the gross stuff. Nobody *really* lives like that."

Now, I keep thinking about the people who'd visited Ann. Those living conditions *hadn't* built up overnight. *Some* of Ann's visitors must have seen what was going on. *Why didn't they say anything?*

Last summer, Henry had kept the apartment clean when he'd lived with Ann and Joe. I remembered Maryann saying that Ann was *furious* when Henry actually moved out, even though Ann had thrown him out. I guess she'd expected him to beg to come back, or something.

Joe had been disappointed, too, because Henry was the only one keeping the apartment livable.

After that… how quickly did it get like what I saw today?

How did the well-groomed prep guy even spend the night there?

What was going on with Joe, when he returned, a few weeks ago? How could he let his son live there? For that matter, how could *Joe* live there?

None of this makes any sense to me.

I'm not sure how quickly Maryann and the rental guys left, after I did. Clearly, they had stronger stomachs than mine.

I just can't believe anyone could live like that. It was like *Hoarders,* at its worst... but this was right next door to me. And, it involved a four-year-old child.

Thursday, November 29th

For three days, people have been inside Ann's apartment, cleaning. It's been pretty noisy, day and night, with them ripping out the carpet — which had been new when Ann moved in — wheeling out the refrigerator, which can't be used again, and so on.

This evening, the last of the maintenance guys was leaving Ann's apartment. I asked him if Ann had removed her belongings.

Nope. The guys had bagged it all up. And, the maintenance guy offered to show me how "good" the apartment looks now, compared with how Ann had left it. So, I got another tour of the apartment.

The kitchen still had some fruit flies. The filth on some of the walls and the baseboard heaters... it's nowhere near as bad as it was, but not even close to clean.

The bedrooms looked pretty good. Kevin's room has new carpeting, and the walls have been painted.

The bathroom door was closed with tape around the edge of the door, like a crime scene.

I asked the guy if he'd taken any before-and-after photos, but he said that he & Erik thought about that too late to get pictures. He said that he can't figure out *why* the sheriff didn't say anything about the living conditions, with a child in the home. I agree.

Even after three days' cleaning, it was like a trip into the Twilight Zone. The guy said there were *thousands* of dead fruit files, stuck to the food residue on the kitchen counters.

They're hiring a special cleaning team for the bathroom. He said they're the kind of cleaners who take care of suicides and crime scenes. Nobody else was willing to deal with it. Good decision.

They're still hoping that Ann comes back for the (now bagged) stuff she left behind. They're giving her until the end of next week to claim her belongings. If her stuff is still there at that point, it goes to the dumpster.

Then they're going to have the entire apartment sealed and treated for bugs, mildew and mold spores.

The guy locked up as we left. He asked me to continue keeping an eye on the apartment, in case Ann tries to get in without permission. Honestly, I have no idea why she'd come back for anything she'd left behind.

I went back to my apartment and stood in the shower for about half an hour, trying to wash the icky feeling off.

Tuesday, December 4th

On Sunday, Ann was here, with a couple of guys and a police escort. Ann took away everything the maintenance guys had bagged. I'm not sure if that's sad or just plain *weird*. I saw absolutely nothing worth keeping. In fact, I'd have piled it all up and *burned* it.

But, speaking of fires...

On Sunday night, someone started a fire in the maintenance shed where they keep the mowers and plowing equipment, and tools for work around the apartments.

Maryann said the police *suspect* it's related to Ann, but they can't prove anything. I guess Ann said something about "getting even" with

Maryann... like any of it was Maryann's fault.

For now, the police are hoping a witness will come forward, but they aren't too optimistic.

Maryann said that Ann is the only recently evicted tenant who was difficult to deal with. And, I guess Ann had been suspected of arson in high school, but nothing was ever proved.

So, all fingers point to Ann, right now... not that it had to be her. We live near a highway, so it could have been *any*one.

Maryann thinks it was just a one-time thing, but she asked me to keep watch for anyone who looks like Ann, or any of her regular visitors like Denise... just in case.

Gosh, will this *ever* end? It's like a bad dream but I can't wake up from it.

They're still working on the apartment next door, trying to make it fit for new tenants. I hear the workers' radio blaring, but that's okay. I put on my own music and work on my next book.

Mostly, I want the past year to fade away so I never even think of Ann again.

People keep writing to me, asking what happened to Kevin and how soon the sequel will come out. I know they want answers. It's kind of gratifying that people care so much about Kevin and his safety.

On the other hand, I'd like to forget this whole thing and get on with my life. My editor asked if I'd be interested in writing a book about islands off the coast of Maine. That sounds like a pretty good project for next spring.

But, I also feel as if I owe closure to the people who've read my earlier book about Kevin.

Saturday, December 28th

I feel like I should keep this diary updated, in

case I decide to publish it, after all. At first, I thought these extra entries — after the first book — would be too brief to publish.

Then, as the story seemed to drag on and on, it's been too depressing to put this together as a book.

Nothing was turning out the way I expected. It wasn't the "happily ever after" ending I wanted.

Back in September, I thought Joe would have full custody of Kevin, and everything would be good for them. I figured Ann would stay here until she was evicted, and use that time to get her life back on track.

Obviously, that's not what happened.

Anyway...

This morning, I brought our rent to the office. While I was there, I asked Maryann if she'd heard anything about Ann, Joe, and Kevin.

I haven't missed them, but I *have* been concerned that Kevin might be even worse off than he was, here.

According to Maryann, Ann has been in the news. She'd moved to a summer community about 40 miles away. (People list their rental cottages and camps, *cheap*, for temporary winter tenants. That's where Ann went.)

Thank heavens, Ann and Kevin managed to move into a duplex with even *nosier* neighbors than me. According to Maryann — who'd read the story in the newspaper — Ann's new neighbors had complained about "the presence of unauthorized male visitors" and a lot of late-night noise.

When the police arrived, Ann wasn't there but two men were, and so was Kevin. While the police were talking with the men, a fire broke out in one bedroom. The newspaper said it was from a "lit, homemade cigarette" left unattended.

The men were arrested on drug charges. Kevin

was taken into custody, and placed in a temporary home. Ann was nowhere to be found.

A few nights later, she showed up at the duplex. Since the landlord had changed the locks, Ann had to break in.

Of course, the neighbors called the police.

Ann was arrested with prescription drugs in her purse... drugs in someone *else's* name. And, she was obviously high and *really* belligerent.

They charged Ann with breaking and entering, possession of drugs, resisting arrest, and suspected prostitution. She was also charged with child endangerment. Her custody rights were temporarily revoked, pending further investigation by DHHS.

At the initial hearing, the prosecutor claimed that Ann was a "flight risk." In other words, Ann might leave town and take Kevin with her. The judge agreed.

So, Ann is in jail.

Joe has Kevin, part time, but there's going to be a psychiatric evaluation — I'm not sure if that's for Joe or Kevin or both — before Joe can keep Kevin overnight.

This isn't over, but I'm feeling much better about everything.

Kevin might finally getting the help he needs. I don't know what the foster care scene is like in New Hampshire, but it's *got* to be better than what Kevin has lived with, so far.

Sunday, March 3rd

Today, after church, a woman asked me if I knew what happened to Ann. That seemed completely out of the blue.

It's been *months* since I'd heard anything about Ann. I assumed that Ann was still in jail and Kevin was with Joe or in foster care. As long as Ann was out of the picture, I've tried not to think about them. For me, it's one of those "things you can't change" issues.

Mostly, the woman wanted to know what happened to Joe and Kevin. She's starting an outreach program for single parents who've been in abusive relationships, and our minister said my former neighbors might be interested.

I told her I'd see what I could find out.

Bleh. I'd like to put an end to questions like that, and the memories they drudge up. But, I'll admit that I *am* curious.

Monday, March 4th

As soon as the office opened this morning, I visited Maryann to see what she knew.

Maryann laughed and said she hasn't thought about Ann and Joe in months, either. She's heard rumors, but she really doesn't care, one way or the other.

She said her sister-in-law is a dispatcher in the town where Ann was arrested, so she'll ask what happened.

Tuesday, March 5th

Apparently, Ann *had* plead guilty to the drug charges and to breaking and entering. She also had a lot of excuses.

I guess they sounded reasonable to the judge, who sentenced Ann to a $350 fine — the minimum — and a year in jail. So, Ann could be out in a few months if she behaves herself.

Maryann said she hasn't any news about Joe yet, and no one seems to know what's going to happen with Kevin, either. Her sister-in-law is pretty sure he's still in foster care.

Friday, March 8th

Maryann always impresses me. I can ask her almost *anything* about local people, and she finds an answer for me. But, she grew up here and I didn't. So, she knows a *lot* more people than I do.

Apparently, Maryann ran into Joe's mom at the grocery store, and quizzed her about the family.

Joe is still in the anger management program, so he still can't get full custody of Kevin. However, he *is* sorry about being a bad father, and he wants to make things right with Kevin.

Joe tried out for a flag football team, and they've invited him to try out for a regional soccer team, too. I didn't realize we had any semi-pro soccer leagues in this area, but — apparently — one has started up, about 45 minutes from here. So, Joe has changed jobs so he can spend time in training with them.

According to Joe's mom — who's pretty proud of Joe for getting back into sports — being on a team has been really good for Joe. He's getting his temper under control, and — at the same time — he's had to clean up his lifestyle. She said the team has a "no tolerance" policy for... well, a lot of things, I guess. So, his mom thinks he's being a better dad when he has time with Kevin.

Joe has a *lot* of growing up to do, and this sounds like a good start.

Joe's parents are looking for a bigger house, maybe with a basement apartment or something. They'd like Joe and Kevin to move in with them, but still have their own space. For now, Joe's mom wants to wait and see how Joe does and if he regains custody, before committing to anything.

Meanwhile, Joe has only a few hours'

supervised time with Kevin, every two weeks. I guess part of that is about Joe's past behavior, but it's also about Kevin's recovery.

The best news is: Kevin has been in really *good* foster care. He's with two or three other kids at a home that's also a horse ranch. The kids get lots of fresh air and they get to help with the horses.

Maryann said that Kevin *loves* it there.

Even better, the foster mom used to be a child psychologist, so the kids get round-the-clock care for anything that's bothering them. And, Kevin is getting plenty of supervision through DHHS. I'm impressed.

Kevin has never had a normal life. This sounds like the best possible way for him to recover. I don't know how long he can stay in that home, but it sounds really good for now.

This is pretty close to the happy ending I wanted for this story.

Saturday, April 27th

I brought the rent check to the office this morning. It's become my monthly check-in with Maryann, catching up on local news. But, this time I gave Maryann our notice. We're moving out in a couple of weeks, and our apartment will be vacant by the end of May.

Maryann said she's sorry that we're moving, but she's glad things are working out for us. She knows we had a pretty rough year when Ann was next door to us. Our new neighbors are a wonderful young couple, but we're ready for our own place now.

Anyway, Maryann said she'd heard from Joe's mother. Ann is up for release in about a few weeks, if she continues to behave herself. The judge says Ann can get out early on several conditions.

First, Ann has to pass a psychiatric evaluation to show that she's no a danger to herself or others. I'm not sure what that is about, but it sounds like a good idea, anyway.

Then, Ann has to relinquish all rights to Kevin. As soon as Ann is released from prison, the judge will sign a restraining order so Ann can't go anywhere near Kevin or the people he's living with.

She can apply for visitation rights in the future, but she has a lot of work to do in the meantime.

Ann also has to get a regular, full-time job. I guess Joe's mom knows someone who manages a local dollar-type store, and he's willing to hire Ann if she's willing to work hard and keep her hand out of the till.

Finally, Ann will have random drug screenings, and have to report at least monthly to a parole officer, showing that she has a job and isn't going back to her old ways.

I'm not convinced that Ann will do what's she's supposed to, but that's not my problem.

Kevin is safe. He's still in the foster home, and the system will see that he's protected. From the start, that was my only real concern.

Monday, May 27th

I think this story is finally over.

Ann *did* get out of jail. I have *no* idea how she convinced the judge that she was ready to be a responsible adult. But, hey, she'd fooled me when we'd chatted on Halloween evening back in 2011, while handing out candy to trick-or-treaters.

According to Joe's mom, Ann has moved to Atlanta, hoping to be cast as an extra in *Vampire Diaries*. I guess Ann is reinventing herself as an actress. Frankly, I think she'd be good at it.

Since Ann left the state without permission,

there *is* a warrant for her arrest. The police know where she is and the name she's using. The Atlanta police know about her, too. If Ann shows up in New Hampshire again, she'll go to jail.

I'm okay with that. I don't wish a *bad* life on Ann. I just want her to stay away from Kevin.

Joe has been on-again, off-again about regaining custody of Kevin. Sometimes he shows up for scheduled visits. Sometimes, he doesn't. His mom says he's pretty busy and needs to grow up a lot more, himself.

He's been seeing a nice young woman who's studying to be a dental assistant. His mom hopes it's a good match for both of them, but she's keeping her distance.

Joe's parents are moving to Florida later this summer. They've bought a mobile home in a nice retirement park. They'd like to have Kevin visit them, but they know nothing is going to change in any hurry. Joe still has a lot of growing up to do, and Joe's mom wants to be sure that Kevin is healthier, too. She still swears that Kevin slapped himself, last October, and she'd never raised a hand to him.

It seemed a *little* odd that she's still talking about that. I don't know what to believe, but I don't really care, either.

Mostly, I wanted to hear about Kevin, but Joe's mom didn't seem to have much news. I'm not sure how often she sees him. She just said that he's still in foster care and he'll be starting school in September.

Then, last week, I was up north for some book research. Before I headed home, I stopped at Walmart for a candy bar.

That's when I saw Kevin myself.

If one of the other kids with him hadn't shouted Kevin's name, I probably wouldn't have recognized him. He's put on weight and — though he always seemed pretty tall for his age — he's grown at least an inch or two. He looks like a normal, healthy five-year-old. (I think he's five years old now, or close to it.)

I'm pretty sure he recognized me. He paused and look a little troubled. I *thought* I saw a brief, "nobody home" look in his eyes, like he was shutting out a memory, followed by a small downward tug at the corner of his mouth.

Then, he seemed to recover. He shouted that he wanted to help push the grocery cart. He ran up to his foster parents, making the same "vroom" noise I used to hear when he was pretending to be a Power Ranger.

He glanced back at me as his new family turned the corner at the end of the store aisle. I think I saw a small smile, but I might be reading into it.

It's a far better outcome than I'd dared to hope for, even a month ago.

From the Author

People often ask me if the Kevin story is true.

Every event in the first book was *exactly* what happened, on the dates they happened, with minor changes (names and descriptions, mostly) to protect the privacy of those involved.

In this second book, I changed more things — especially dates and the context of some events — so people won't put the two books together and figure out who Ann, Joe, and Kevin are. For example, "Denise" was actually two different women, but — in this book — I combined them into one character.

The most *awful* things in this book — including the abuse, Kevin trying to climb over the side of his balcony, and the filth Ann left behind in the apartment — were just as bad as I described.

What's important is that Kevin is safe, Joe is trying to be a responsible dad, and Ann is hundreds of miles away... and not likely to return to New Hampshire.

All of that is completely true, and I hope that puts your mind at rest.

Handshake King was probably an undercover police officer. Apparently, he was working on a case related to child pornography. The drug dealing was a smokescreen.

Pippi turned her life around, found a truly good man, and married him. Last time I saw her, I didn't recognize her. She had to tell me who she was. Her "bad girl" image is a thing of the past. I was glad to see her so happy.

Readers have also asked about me... my life, my career, my family, and so on.

My husband got a promotion and we've moved to our own home in a different NH town. That's made a *huge* difference in our lives.

One of our kids started college at the start of this summer. She's a little nervous to be away from home, but excited about her future. Our other two children are — like her — happy that their mom and dad aren't woken up nightly by an abusive neighbor.

I'm happy to say my writing career is back on track, too.

So, we're *all* doing better.

I wish I'd been able to help Kevin sooner. I also hope New Hampshire laws will change. It *should* be easier for the police to intervene when they know abuse is going on.

As the economy improves, I hope DHHS gets more funding and staff, so they can assess cases like Kevin's, and do more to help children at risk.

I've discussed Kevin's case with my former minister and a woman who's running the support group for single parents. They're looking for better ways to help that community. They're sure other children are being abused and falling through the cracks in the system.

As of early 2013, my first book about Kevin's plight had sold over 15,000 copies and many readers have written to me. Some emails have been mean-spirited, but most of them have been deeply touching. Many come from social services workers all over the U.S., who tell me that most states share the same kinds of problems as New Hampshire.

I never expected my first book to sell a single copy.

Since publishing that book, I *have* heard from politicians who've said they're looking for better answers, too. I'm glad to hear that.

Mostly, I'm relieved that Kevin is in a safe, happy home now. He's getting the care that he needs. He has a chance to grow up strong and healthy.

It's closer to "happily ever after" than I'd dared to hope for.

What you can do

If you were moved by Kevin's story, I hope you'll look into *your* community's resources for troubled families. As I learned the hard way, most communities and states don't have the resources they need to assess and help *every* case brought to their attention, even the desperate ones. Often, they have to settle for helping the very worst cases... and many of them are far more dangerous than Kevin's home was.

In my opinion, our society is in trouble and *there are no easy answers*. We're a couple of generations past the era when a parent was always there to welcome a child home from school.

In fact, many of today's young parents were raised by a single mom or dad working multiple jobs to make ends meet. They don't necessarily know how to be good parents, themselves. "Getting by" isn't always enough, especially when a child has behavioral issues or special needs.

Too often, parents like Ann and Joe have *no idea* how to deal with family problems, and *not a clue* where to *begin* to find help. Churches and community centers can be great resources, but only if young parents have time to visit them, and feel comfortable doing so.

I believe that the answer isn't just to throw more money at state agencies. Many of them *do* need more help, but the problem is more systemic than that. It's at the core of our society. It's the result of stress and excessive demands on families' time and finances.

Others have talked about this problem — and

possible grass-roots solutions — with better insights than I have.

I hope my books have shown that getting help for a child in trouble... it's not as simple as calling the police or even your state's family services offices.

Please, do what you can for a young family near you. If we each get to know our neighbors and stay in touch with our extended families, we can make a difference, a little at a time.

To Report Child Abuse or Neglect in NH

To contact the office of the NH Department of Health & Humans Services, Child Protective Services, contact 800-894-5533 (in state only), or 603-271-6562 (out of state) 8:00 AM. to 4:30 PM, Monday thru Friday. That reaches the intake office of the Division of Children, Youth, and Families.

However, as of 2012, it said at their webpage (http://www.dhhs.state.nh.us/dcyf/cps/index.htm), "DCYF receives more than 15,000 reports of suspected child abuse and neglect annually... Approximately 8,000 reports are assessed annually in NH."

In other words, slightly more than 50% of reported cases of abuse are assessed each year.

If your report is one of approximately *7,000 that aren't assessed,* you're not alone in your frustration. Continue to report the situation. With increased reports, the odds improve so the abused and/or neglected child has a better chance of receiving help.

Meanwhile, start looking for — or build — a local support system to prevent child abuse and neglect, and help families who aren't able to cope. In fact, every community should have several systems working together, including faith-based outreach when abuse or neglect are suspected.

The existing state system is overburdened. Shifting even more responsibility and blame onto them is not helpful. Help is more likely to come from people we know and see every day, for people we know and see every day.

In a 2007 statewide survey of victims of abuse, more than 70% of NH men reported a history that

includes physical assault
(http://www.nhcadsv.org/uploads/VAM
%20Report%20Final.pdf). That's higher than the
national average.

Among males who'd been physically assaulted,
34% of the perpetrators were women.

Those numbers surprised me. I thought I knew
a lot about child abuse and neglect, but I didn't.
Greater awareness can help individuals better
recognize family problems when they see them.

Preventing child abuse and neglect isn't
someone else's problem. It's rarely an issue that
can be fully resolved by one person... not you, not
me, and not someone with a desk and a title.
That's especially true when his or her office is
understaffed, underpaid, given limited latitude to
take action, and overloaded with cases.

However, none of us can look the other way. As
individuals, if we each do a little — as much as we
can without compromising the time we need for
our own families — we can make a difference.

Kevin's case was not unique. Chances are, you
know a family in distress or a child who is being
abused. I hope this book inspires action on your
part, to protect the Kevins in your community, and
make sure systems exist to help families trapped in
patterns of abuse.

About the Author

Shannon Bowen is a wife, and the mother of three wonderful children. She's also a travel writer, and she's active with her church.

Her other book about Kevin is called *Momma, Don't Hit Me!*
Both stories -- complete -- are combined in the two-book compilation, *"What Happened to Kevin."*

With a friend, Shannon as co-authored *The Wicked Widow,* a story about marital betrayal.

You can contact Shannon at her website, Shannon-Bowen.com.